The First Crusade (1096-1099)

PRUSSIANS

LITHUANIA

GDANSK

KINGDOM
OF
POLAND

PRINCIPALTIY
OF
KIEV

KIEV

KINGDOM
OF
HUNGARY

BLACK SEA

BELGRAD

DOM
F
BIA

NISH

TURNOVO

PHILIPPOLIS

CONSTANTINOPPLE

SINOP

ANATOLIA

OCHRIDA

KOMATUHA

ADRIANOPLE

NICAEA

DORYLAEUM

CAESAREA

MARA

HERACLEA

EDESSA

TARSUS

AEGEAN
SEA

ANTIOCH

MARRA

RHODES

TRIPOLI

CYPRUS

TURE

DAMASCUS

ACRE

TIBERIAS

CRETE

JAFFA

ASCALON

JERUSALEM

DAMIETTA

ALEXANDRIA

CAIRO

CAIRO

The Crusades

Acknowledgments

The publisher AeroArt International would like to thank several people without whose skills and help this book would not have been possible. Thanks to Yli Remo Vallejo's scholarly interest in history and research of material, text for this 200-year duration of The Crusades is lively and entertaining. We would like to thank our photographer, graphics artist, and technical advisor Tor Johnson for his multi-faceted contributions. Thanks to Kristie Matthews our graphics artist for her very creative and visual ideas throughout. Thanks also to Carol Sirkus whose professional guidance enabled us to correctly say what we needed to say, Nancy Fernandez who typed each chapter more times than anyone would want to, Gudrun Johnson for her proofreading expertise, and Russ Salberg for being available to discuss historical events.

In Russia, we would like to thank Igor Dzis for his beautiful illustrations. Thanks to our associate Elena Levicheva at Rosman Publishing and to our Russian chargé d'affaires Svetlana Iakovleva — a very capable businesswoman and friend.

AeroArt International, Inc.

Text by Yli Remo Vallejo
Illustrated by Igor Dzis
Edited by Thor Johnson

Design by Tor Johnson and Kristie Matthews
Printed and bound by Elway Lithograph, Sterling, Virginia

The Crusades

By Yli Remo Vallejo
Illustrated by Igor Dzis

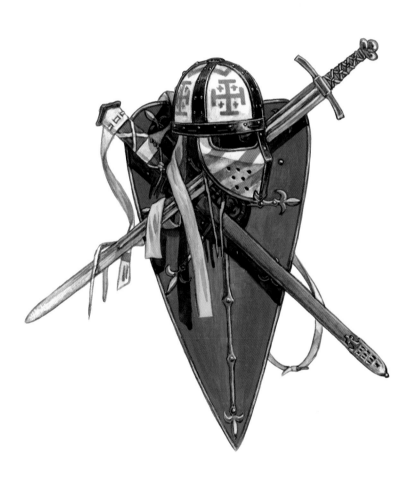

AeroArt International, Inc.
Great Falls, Virginia
2002

Publisher's Foreword

AeroArt International produces the highest quality connoisseur historical miniatures known as The St. Petersburg Collection. In the course of creating museum-grade figures for collectors, we are constantly in search of reference material to guide us in the production of historically authentic figures. It is with this research in mind that we have chosen to publish this book on the eight famous Crusades.

Two years ago on a business trip to St. Petersburg, Russia, in connection with a new line of crusader-period figures we were planning to introduce, I met with one of our award-winning artists. It was a cold, blustery day in St. Petersburg; and between sips of hot Russian coffee, we discussed weapons and costumes of crusader knights of the twelfth and thirteenth centuries. During our conversation the artist removed from his briefcase a Russian language book on the subject of the Crusades. I was extremely impressed with the beautiful illustrations of the famous battles, sieges, and personalities of the many crusades. After seeing this exciting book, I investigated the possibility of obtaining the rights for U.S. publication. The results of discussions with the Russian publisher are seen here.

To meet the requirements of the English-language market, we had the book completely rewritten and added pictures of "The St. Petersburg Collection" crusader figures to provide more illustrations of this fascinating historical period. Collectors of our award-winning miniatures will recognize many of the inspirations for our crusader and Saracen figures.

We are extremely proud of the quality of this initial venture into publishing, and we believe this abbreviated history of the Crusades and the attendant illustrations will substantially captivate your imagination and enhance your historic collection and reading pleasure.

Thor Johnson

Thor Johnson
President
AeroArt International

Contents

The First Crusade: The Christian Victory 1096—1099

"All over Europe, men, women, and children prepared to march to the Holy Land to confront the infidels. Nobles leased their lands to finance the sacred expedition; monks prepared to leave their monasteries; and the lower classes left for the long journey with no more than a few days' provisions."

In the second half of the eleventh century, three cultures were moving headlong toward a violent collision whose echoes still reverberate today. Then, as today, Jerusalem was the bloody crossroads.

Jerusalem, the city of prophets, the navel of the world, and birthplace of three religions, had been in Muslim hands since 638 A.D. The new conquerors, with tolerance uncharacteristic of the era, ensured that the Christian and Jewish residents enjoyed the freedom to practice their religions. Over the succeeding three centuries, Muslim hegemony in the Middle East, North Africa, and Spain disintegrated with schisms, regionalism, and tribalism creating a patchwork of emirates linked by faith in Allah and mutual distrust.

The remnants of the Roman Empire, the Byzantine power residing in Constantinople, maintained its tenuous control over the Balkans, Greece, and Anatolia (latter-day Turkey east of the Bosphorus). It was a mature power with a developed culture, characterized now as Eastern Orthodox, which had evolved over several centuries of estrangement from Western Europe and its Dark Ages.

Western Europe, still culturally backward compared to the Muslim and Byzantine societies, was also a patchwork quilt of competing interests. The Norman ascendancy culminated in the conquest of England in 1066 and the colonization of southern Italy and Sicily. Western Europe was the stage for the often-violent struggle between the pope and his supposed protector, the Holy Roman Emperor, who was essentially the king of the German-speaking Teutonic regions. The French feudal lords were divided regionally, with the king of France a distant, and for now, irrelevant entity.

There was a peace that marked the relations among these three centers—a peace born of distance and disinterest rather than interaction and understanding. The arrival of the Seljuk Turks from the East upset this calm.

Seljuks

The Seljuks were a Turkish tribe who migrated from Asia and converted to Islam along the way. By the mid-eleventh century, they had begun to move from Persia to wrest control of the eastern Muslim world from the caliph of Baghdad, the Fatimids of Egypt, and the various autonomous emirs. All these would swear fealty to the Seljuk sultan. Even Jerusalem would be ruled by a Turkish governor.

The Seljuk expansion inevitably reached north to Byzantine Anatolia. On August 19, 1071, Byzantine Emperor Roman IV Diogenes (1068–1071) met the invading Seljuk-led Muslim army commanded by Sultan Alp Arslan outside the fortified town of Manzikert. The Seljuks took to their usual tactic—feigning retreat, they suddenly attacked the Byzantine flanks with their heavy cavalry. The army of Roman IV was almost entirely destroyed, and the emperor himself was thrown down at the feet of the Turkish sultan. Anatolia and its Christian populace passed into Muslim rule. Jerusalem fell to the Turks the next year.

Sultan Alp Arslan's son, Malik Shah, eventually ruled this greatest empire of its time; but upon his death in 1092, the Seljuk kingdom disintegrated into competing emirates. Western Anatolia known as Rum ("Rome") was ruled by Malik Shah's brother, Kilij Arslan. By the time of the First Crusade, the Seljuks were in decline. The Egyptian Fatimids would recapture Jerusalem in advance of the Frankish armies, but the lack of a strong unifying sultan allowed the Europeans to prevail against foes riven by mutual suspicion.

Pope Urban's Call to Crusade

In 1095 Byzantine Emperor Alexius Comnenus (1081–1118) sent a delegation to Pope Urban II (1088–1099) requesting assistance from the Western powers to recover his Anatolian lands from the Seljuk sultan. Although the request never included the recapture of Jerusalem, Urban used it as a pretext to call for a holy war by Christian warriors to recapture Jerusalem and the Holy Land. The pope announced this quite eloquently outside Clermont Cathedral in south central France, promising forgiveness of sins to

those who fought the non-Christian Saracens. God's soldiers were to wear a red cross sewn on their tunics. Urban tore his own red cloak to be made into these holy badges.

Pilgrimages to the Holy Land were not infrequent in the eleventh century despite the distances involved and the primitive system of roads. Although harassment by brigands was a given peril, there had been no systematic persecution of Christian visitors to the Holy Land except for the few years (1009–1021) when the insane Fatimid caliph of Egypt, al-Hakim, targeted Jews and Christians with cruel and capricious laws. The disintegration of the Seljuk's authority increased the criminal peril to travelers; however, religious tolerance still prevailed in the Holy City of Jerusalem. Urban's creative description of the torture and rape of Christians, including Saracens roasting Christian babies on spits, unleashed a frenzy of passion and hatred that appeared to unite the competing factions of Western Christendom. "Deus volt!" ("God wills it!") was the rallying cry.

All over Europe, men, women, and children prepared to march to the Holy Land to confront the infidels. Nobles leased their lands to finance the sacred expedition; monks prepared to leave their monasteries; and the lower classes left for the long journey with no more than a few days' provisions. Although Urban appointed Adhemar, bishop of Puy, as his personal representative who would travel with the crusaders, there was effectively no central control of this vast body of Europeans acting on the pope's call to arms for a Holy Crusade.

Three major armed contingents began to organize: the German group from the Holy Roman Empire under Godfrey de Bouillon and his younger brothers, Eustace and Baldwin; the French under Raymond of Toulouse; and the Italo-Normans led by Bohemond de Hauteville of Otranto and his nephew, Tancred. Smaller contingents would be loosely associated with these groups. Among them was Robert of Normandy, son of the late William the Conqueror and brother of King William Rufus of England, and his brother-in-law Stephen of Blois.

Above: A Byzantine soldier in Turkish captivity after Manzikert.
Picture previous page: The Seljuk Turks defeat the Byzantine army at the Battle of Manzikert in 1071.

Leaders of the First Crusade

The First Crusade was the only successful crusade. The recapture of Jerusalem was accomplished despite the competing egos of five leaders who commanded three separate armies:

French

Raymond of Toulouse (1041–1105)

The wealthiest and most important of the great knights who took up the cross and went on a crusade was Raymond of Toulouse. Raymond was an old man in his fifties when he left for the Holy Land. History considers him the best military mind among the leaders of the First Crusade as he studied Saracen tactics and devised his own countermeasures. His instincts may have been honed by his years of campaigning against the Moors in Spain. He founded the principality pf Tripoli, now most of modern-day Lebanon. He died in 1105 in his castle outside Tripoli.

German (Holy Roman Empire)

Godfrey of Bouillon, Duke of Lower Lorraine (1061–1100)

Godfrey was in his mid-thirties when he led his regiments of German knights and followers. He descended from Charlemagne on his mother's side and was a member of the family of the Counts of Boulogne. He was an even-tempered voice of reason among the many leaders of the First Crusade. A humble and reserved man who had fought in two wars, he had a warrior's physical strength to complement his quiet leadership. Godfrey became the first Frank ruler of Jerusalem in 1099 although he shunned the title of king. He died a year after Jerusalem fell, possibly from poisoned food offered by Saracens at a peace parley.

Baldwin of Boulogne (1068–1118)

The youngest of the three brothers, Baldwin was a landless noble in search of fortune and power. He certainly found both in this armed pilgrimage. On the way to Jerusalem he split from the German forces to capture Edessa and became the ruler of this first crusader principality. He succeeded his brother and became King Baldwin I of Jerusalem and consolidated Western hold on Palestine. After an eighteen year reign, marked by constant battle with the Saracens and rival Franks, Baldwin died in 1118. A touching story survives regarding Baldwin. As he crossed the Jordan, upon hearing the moans of a Muslim woman in childbirth, he stopped to protect her with his rain cloak and ordered fruit and water to be laid on her prayer rug. When the woman gave birth, he sent a camel to provide milk and a slave woman to accompany her and the child as they traveled home. Unknown to Baldwin, the woman's husband was an emir. That same emir later repaid Baldwin's kindness by helping Baldwin escape when he was trapped in Ramlah by a large Egyptian army.

Italo-Normans

Bohemond of Otranto, Count of Apulia (1050–1111)

Bohemond was a member of the Norman de Hauteville clan who a generation earlier had taken over southern Italy and Sicily. The family, under his father Robert Guiscard and his uncle Roger, supported the pope in his various conflicts. In return, the pope granted the legitimacy of Norman rule over the Italian lands they had invaded. Bohemond helped restore Urban to the papal throne in Rome in 1094. Of all the principal leaders, Bohemond was the most ambitious for personal gain, having limited family resources behind him. In his forties when he arrived in Constantinople, he made quite an impression on Anna Comnenus, the Byzantine emperor's daughter, who described him in the pages of her history as a tall, perfect physical embodiment of the Nordic warrior, cultured and well behaved but with a quiet warlike mien. After the taking of Antioch, he stayed behind and became its prince. Subsequently, a Turkish emir captured him in 1100, and in 1103 he was ransomed. He returned to Europe to raise a crusade against the Byzantines but was soundly defeated in battle. He finally retired to his southern Italian estate where he died in 1111.

Tancred de Hauteville (1076–1112)

Tancred accompanied his uncle Bohemond but switched his allegiance to Godfrey of Bouillon. He was only twenty-one years of age at the start of the Crusades. A fierce fighter, he was among the first to enter Jerusalem. After this victory, he was granted land in Galilee and was appointed regent of Antioch by his uncle. He fought to preserve Frankish gains until 1112 when he died of typhus. He was only thirty-six.

"The moral underpinnings of the Crusades had quickly dissolved to reveal the awakened hatred of anyone non-Roman Catholic, anyone non-Western European, anyone different."

Ahead of these armies departed a large, ill-fated ragtag rabble of peasants, priests, armed nobles, and men-at-arms who followed a charismatic preacher named Peter the Hermit. Eloquent preachers fanned the fervor sparked by Urban, and none was more eloquent than Peter the Hermit who found himself leading an eager mob. Peter has been depicted in medieval illustrations as a typical monk with the shaved tonsure wearing crude hooded monk's robes. An ascetic whose diet consisted of fish and wine, he inspired devotion and veneration. His followers even pulled the hairs from his mule to keep as relics.

Peter the Hermit and the Peasants' Crusade

Urban's call to arms was meant for the armed classes: the nobility and their men-at-arms. However, the stirring depiction of Christianity debased and the promise of expiation of one's sins roused an unexpected and enthusiastic response from the peasant class. Whether driven by the hope of a better life in Palestine or the righteousness of their religious cause, the poor prepared to leave their wretched homes. Most of the men on whom the women and children depended for safety were untrained in soldiery.

Peter led fourteen thousand people, followed by an equal number of northern French Christians led by Walter sans Avoir (Walter the Penniless), and another six thousand under the French knight, Fulcher of Orleans. A group of German knights and peasants from the Rhine region could not wait for the main armed regiments already forming and left in April 1096 joining Peter's zealous peasantry. Passing through Germany, Hungary, and Bulgaria, they pillaged villages for supplies, killing inhabitants who resisted, and

massacred Jews, even those protected by local bishops. Evidence of these pogroms can still be found in Worms, Mainz, Regensburg, and Cologne. The moral underpinnings of the Crusades had quickly dissolved to reveal the awakened hatred of anyone non-Roman Catholic, anyone non-Western European, anyone different. Over the two centuries of crusades, the Franks would kill almost as many eastern Christians and Jews as Saracens.

Peter the Hermit's marauding bands incurred great losses in skirmishes with local troops and armed peasants. Still, they accounted for the killing of four thousand in the Hungarian border town of Semlin and the sacking and burning of Belgrade. The Byzantines fearfully dreaded the rivers of foreigners streaming toward them. Upon their arrival on August 1, Emperor Alexius Comnenus barred their entry into Constantinople, a city bigger and richer than any these loathsome savages had seen in the Western world. Alexius immediately dispatched them to Asia Minor along with requested supplies, but not before they engaged in more mischief. For six days outside the city walls, these "holy pilgrims" looted homes and skirmished with Byzantine soldiers.

Upon being ferried across to Anatolia, the great bulk of Peter's rabble continued to ravage indigenous villages sparing neither Christian nor Turk in their quest for booty. Within this mass of thousands of pilgrims, regional European conflicts developed. Fraying along national lines, French quarreled with Germans and Italians forcing separate encampments. Germans and Italians camped at Xerigordon Castle near the capital of Nicaea (present day Isnik); the French camped by the sea at Civetot. Xerigordon was besieged by a Turkish force to which the Germans and Italians surrendered in eight days, having to choose between conversion to Islam or death. Meanwhile, the French were lured out of their camp; and on October 21, 1096, the Saracens attacked and killed twenty-five thousand Christians. Walter the Penniless was killed; Peter the Hermit was spared as he had returned to Constantinople for help and escaped the onslaught. Many pilgrims fell captive and were sold into slavery leaving three thousand to emerge from the slaughter. Some returned home and others stayed to wait for the arrival of the organized armed contingents already on the move. The crusade of Peter the Hermit was thus ended.

The First Crusade Begins

In August 1096, a large regiment commanded by Godfrey of Bouillon, and accompanied by his brothers, Eustace, Count of Boulogne, and Baldwin, set out from Lotharingia bound for the Holy Land with banners flying from spear tips. Soon thereafter, the French under Raymond of Toulouse, the Italo-Normans under Bohemond with his nephew Tancred, and the Anglo-Normans led by Robert of Normandy and Stephen of Blois all began their own separate journeys that would stop at Constantinople before crossing into Asia Minor.

Byzantine Emperor Alexius met the leaders of each contingent as they arrived at his capital, showered them with gifts, and required an oath from each to become his liegeman in exchange for supplies and support. Although a small group under Hugh of Vermandois was the first to arrive, Godfrey's was the first major force to reach Constantinople. Godfrey refused to swear an oath of homage to the emperor and a standoff ensued. No oath, no food. Godfrey unleashed an assault on the city and demanded Alexius to rescind his conditions. During the course of the fighting, the Franks treacherously attacked Alexius' messengers, causing Alexius to send additional forces to battle with Godfrey. Godfrey, fearing irreplaceable casualties to his army, relented and finally swore the oath of allegiance.

Bohemond's Italo-Norman contingent and Raymond's French forces arrived in Constantinople soon after. Like Peter's peasant army, these warring factions hewed a violent path through the Balkans. Upon meeting the Byzantine emperor, Bohemond demanded that Alexius grant to him command of all

The crusaders commandeer supplies from Balkan villages.
Here a Jew is robbed while the evening dinner is harvested.

military forces in Byzantium and Asia Minor. The emperor refused Bohemond's demands but convinced Bohemond nevertheless to swear an oath of fealty to him.

The three main armies finally gathered together on the east side of the Bosphorus, creating a total of sixty thousand fighting men plus their households and followers. This gathered Christian host vowed to free the holy places from the hands of the nonbelievers. Peter the Hermit and the other clerics traveling with the armies offered prayers and blessings for the journey.

The Siege of Nicaea

The city of Nicaea was the capital of Rum (most of modern-day Turkey), home to Kilij Arslan, Turkish ruler of Anatolia. The city was an important center in the history of early Christianity. The statement of beliefs, the Nicene Creed, still prayed by today's Catholics, was formulated here. The city sits on the shores of Lake Ascan that connects to the Sea of Marmara. Wide double walls with 370 stone towers protect it. Godfrey blockaded the city from the north, Bohemond from the east, and Raymond from the south. The city walls bordered the lake on the southwest, and the crusaders had no boats to block this access.

A few days into the siege, a large Turkish cavalry army of fifty thousand led by Kilij Arslan rode down from the mountains and began the first mounted battle of the Crusades. The battle featured contrasting styles of mounted warfare. The Franks on war stallions organized themselves into ordered masses and thundered into the enemy with lances couched. The Turks, on their nimble mares, charged in loose groups launching arrows and then wheeled away. Both sides inflicted heavy casualties. In the end, the Turks withdrew.

The siege could have lasted longer than the endured six weeks had it not been for the shrewd intervention of the Byzantine emperor. Although they still received supplies by water, the Turks began to feel the effects of the siege. Alexius persuaded Kilij Arslan to surrender to him, assuring protection for Arslan's family and preservation of the city from the customary post-siege sack and plunder. Byzantine troops arrived by boat one night, and the crusaders awoke the next dawn perplexed and frustrated to see Byzantine flags

Picture to left: Battle of Nicaea.

flying from the ramparts of Nicaea. Alexius pacified the Franks with gold and other spoils. An additional bonus for Alexius was an oath of fealty from Tancred (Bohemond's nephew) and the recovery of the city of Smyrna from the Turks. Alexius' political astuteness only helped feed the growing prejudice the Franks held against the Byzantines.

Battle of Dorylaeum

The combined host soon regrouped and headed toward Palestine, traversing unmapped country over unpaved roads and unmarked trails. After two days they divided into two groups as they made their way across the desert. Godfrey of Bouillon, Raymond of Toulouse, and Robert of Flanders proceeded along the coastal route. The other group, led by Bohemond, Tancred, and Robert of Normandy, traveled the inland route.

On the plain of Dorylaeum, Bohemond suddenly found himself under attack by Kilij Arslan who had gathered a new force after Nicaea. Although Bohemond and Tancred were quick to establish a strong defensive position by a lake, the Turks were too numerous. On the verge of collapse, Bohemond was rescued by the timely appearance of Godfrey's corps who attacked the Turks from the rear. The Turks fled from the vise, leaving weapons, horses, and tents full of plunder for the crusaders. This utter defeat removed the Anatolian Turks as a major impediment to the crusaders' military progress and future success.

The crusaders still faced other barriers: the terrain, the weather, meager supplies, and a few more hostile fortresses—the strongest of which was Antioch.

The Approach to Antioch: Crusader Fights Crusader

To enter Syria and reach Palestine from Asia Minor, the most direct route followed the meandering coast across the Taurus Mountains through the Cilician Gates, a mountain pass offering perfect ambush country. The crusaders labored in the August heat in the harsh, dry country of the Taurus foothills. Many died of thirst. Beasts of burden perished. Proud knights became foot soldiers. When they reached Heraclea at the entrance to the Cilician Gates, all except a small force decided to turn toward the northeast, away from the direction of Jerusalem, to make use of the paved Byzantine road through more verdant and friendly Armenian Christian territory. They would then turn south to cross the Anti-Taurus Mountains and approach Antioch from the east.

The Armenians, subjugated by both the Byzantines and the Turks, saw the crusaders as liberators. Crusaders Baldwin (Godfrey's brother) and Tancred saw in the Armenians an opportunity for power and fortune. On the other side of the Cilician Gates was the Armenian town of Tarsus, St. Paul's birthplace. Tancred was assured that its citizens would attack the Turkish garrison upon his arrival. With the blessing of his uncle, Bohemond, Tancred took one hundred knights and two hundred foot soldiers through the Cilician Gates, but he could not defeat the Turks at Tarsus. A second group of five hundred knights and two thousand infantry led by Baldwin came through the pass causing the Turks to flee. This force was not sent to help Tancred but to check his ambition. Tancred had no choice but to let Baldwin conquer Tarsus. When a new group of Bohemond's followers arrived a few days later, Baldwin refused them entry to the city, thus allowing the pursuing Turks who were still a military presence outside the city to massacre the small force.

The favorite tactic of Muslim cavalry was a quick charge to release their arrows and a rapid retreat.

Frankish warriors defending themselves against Turkish horse archers.

When Tancred turned west to capture more Armenian towns from the Turks, Baldwin followed until the two groups of crusaders fought each other at Mamistra. A truce was agreed to, and both sides withdrew.

The main crusader group found that the expected safety and comfort of the Byzantine road through the Anti-Taurus range now disappeared into steep paths atop terrifying crags made muddy and slippery by October rains. Men and horses fell into chasms, and wagons slipped down precipices. By the time they reached the plains on the other side, this army had lost at least a fourth of its strength.

Baldwin Becomes the Count of Edessa

Baldwin, who had shadowed Tancred through the Cilician Gates, met the haggard main army coming down from the Anti-Taurus slopes. Faced with the death of his wife, his only tenuous link to wealth, Baldwin sought a new avenue to repair his fortune and determined to capture the city of Edessa. Baldwin and one hundred knights hastily rode to that Armenian principality more than 100 miles to the east on the banks of the Euphrates River. Edessa, a thriving city surrounded by Turkish emirates, survived only because the feuding emirs resented each other more than the innocuous Christian community in their midst. The crusaders were welcomed as allies by their fellow Christians of Edessa.

Baldwin demanded that Thoros, the governor of Edessa, designate him as his heir. This required a rite of adoption that was originally intended for infants. To fulfill this rite of adoption, Baldwin rubbed bare breasts with each of his adoptive parents within the confines of a blanket. Less than a month after this strange rite, Thoros was killed in a revolt, and his heir Baldwin established the first Western European principality. Edessa would guard the crusaders' eastern flank for almost fifty years.

The Siege of Antioch

Antioch was an impressively fortified city surrounded by 18 miles of double walls guarded by 450 towers. Its walls, wide enough for four horses abreast, rose with the mountains to the south and extended to the summit of Mt. Silpius, which was crowned with an imposing citadel overlooking the city below.

The crusaders did not have enough men to surround the massive complex. Food was limited. However, starvation would not be an immediate weapon because within the surrounding walls were pastures and farmland. Despite the formidable task, the ragged army of crusaders laid siege to Antioch. Each contingent besieged a portion of the northeast sector. Bohemond camped outside St. Paul's Gate; Raymond deployed his troops a mile from Bohemond's right at the Gate of the Dog. Godfrey stationed his soldiers to Raymond's right to guard the Gate of the Duke. The balance of the army waited in reserve. The rest of the walled city went unguarded as the crusaders waited and suffered outside Antioch's walls, short on food in the cold rains of winter. The crusaders had no siege engines to mount a proper assault on the city. Turkish raiding parties would ride out of the city to harass Christians on their daily forage for food. Even a massive foraging expedition of twenty thousand led by Bohemond and Robert of Flanders far into Muslim territory yielded little. By the end of winter, at least one man out of seven in the Christian army had died of starvation. Many deserted, including Peter the Hermit, who was chased back to the crusader camp by Tancred.

In the crusader ranks there were priests who blamed the Christians' suffering on the women of the camps, saying licentiousness the women evoked

CAPTURE OF ANTIOCH

ROBERT OF NORMANDY

BOHEMOND

ROBERT OF FLANDERS

RAYMOND OF TOULOUSE

GODFREY

⬦—⬦	Crusader Fortifications
▬	Crusader Infantry
▬	Crusader Cavalry
①	Crusader forces repelling Seljuk cavalry attack
②	Detachment of Bohemond's forces deflecting sorties of Garrison units
▬	Town Garrison
⌐	Seljuk forces blockading the town

brought God's wrath upon the crusader army. To cleanse the armies of lust and fornication and to win God's favor anew, all women married or not were driven out of the camps. The women awaited the outcome of the siege in a nearby fortified settlement.

Fearing an eventual crusader victory at Antioch, Turkish Governor Yaghi-Siyan appealed to the rulers of Damascus and Aleppo for help. The small forces they sent were beaten back by the European besiegers. In the early spring a small English fleet commanded by Edgar Aetheling, a pretender to the English throne, arrived at nearby St. Symeon with much needed supplies, siege machines, and wood for siege fortifications. A contingent of English mercenaries from the Byzantine emperor's Varangian Guard provided welcome reinforcements. Meanwhile, Kerbogha, the powerful emir of Mosul, was gathering the largest army that the crusaders would encounter.

In the end Antioch fell, not by force but by treachery. Bohemond conspired with a disaffected Armenian Muslim convert named Firouz whose wife had been seduced by a local garrison commander. As Kerbogha approached, Firouz let down a ladder from the Tower of the Two Sisters allowing the crusaders to finally enter Antioch. With the help of Christians within the city, the gates were opened to the besiegers; and the city of Antioch fell on June 3, 1098. The crusaders slaughtered any Turks they met and, in the confusion, some Christians as well. A small number of Turks reached the citadel at Mt. Silpius where they watched streets fill with corpses as the Christians conducted a proper looting rampage. Yaghi-Siyan's severed head oversaw the blood orgy.

Kerbogha arrived too late to save Antioch, because he first attempted to drive Baldwin out of Edessa before coming to Antioch's aid. Baldwin held fast in Edessa and Kerbogha eventually left for Antioch. Despite Bohemond's attacks, the citadel overlooking the city of Antioch was still in Turkish hands when Kerbogha's army arrived. However, the besiegers now became the besieged as Kerbogha had enough men to cover all of the city's gates. The crusaders again found themselves on the brink of annihilation with a large enemy force outside of Antioch's walls, while the citadel's Turkish garrison threatened them from within. Despite disease burning their bones and starvation gnawing at their bellies, the crusaders fought on. With the outcome of the battle still in doubt, the Christian ships in St. Symeon harbor

set sail to escape. With food gone and prospects for victory dim, desertions increased dramatically. Stephen of Blois and a group of deserters in their flight from Antioch encountered the Byzantine Emperor Alexius I and a military contingent crossing Anatolia headed for Antioch and the relief of the embattled crusaders. To cover up their cowardly act, the deserters convinced the emperor that all was lost in Antioch, and that any rescue attempt would be too late. The emperor and his troops returned to Constantinople.

The crusaders, now trapped in Antioch, needed a miracle. In the midst of their despair, the miracles began. A drunkard peasant named Peter Bartholomew approached Raymond of Toulouse and Bishop Adhemar le Puy, the papal legate, and recounted a remarkable dream. St. Andrew had revealed to him in a series of visions that the Holy Lance that pierced Christ's side was buried in Antioch's cathedral. Others, too, had visions. A priest named Stephen reported that Jesus had told him that if the crusaders turned from sin, within five days God would send a mighty host to help conquer their enemies. The excavation of the cathedral recovered nothing until Peter Bartholomew himself jumped into the pit and retrieved a rusty lance head. Sufficiently inspired, the bishop declared a three-day fast to cleanse their souls (an easy thing in

Above: The Saracens mounted on mares would charge in loose groups, launching arrows, and wheeling away.

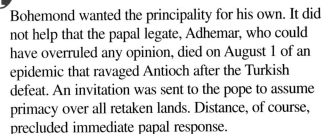

the absence of food). On June 28, at the end of the fast and after a solemn mass, the gates of the city were opened. The ailing Raymond of Toulouse watched as one hundred weary mounted knights somehow routed the large Turkish army. With the Holy Lance at their head, the Christians swore that they saw heavenly warriors coming down, multiplying their strength. The Turkish army fled before the onslaught. In reality Peter Bartholomew was suspected even by many crusaders of planting a rusted spearhead in the pit of Antioch Cathedral.

Kerbogha's army was comprised of levies from various emirates of Persia, Syria, and Palestine. The resentful emirs were beset with internal divisions. They could not bear to give the hated Kerbogha a victory over the Franks and thus achieve more fame and power. When the entire crusader army came forth to meet in battle, the Turkish emirs who distrusted Kerbogha withdrew their forces from the field of conflict and went home.

The March to Jerusalem

After more than eight months at Antioch, the road to Jerusalem, less than 400 miles south, now lay wide open. The most powerful of Muslim armies had been defeated. Still the exhausted crusader army tarried at Antioch, its leaders unsure of their next move. A dispute over the control of the fortress arose between Raymond of Toulouse and Bohemond. Raymond insisted that the city be turned over to the Byzantine emperor according to the vows they had taken;

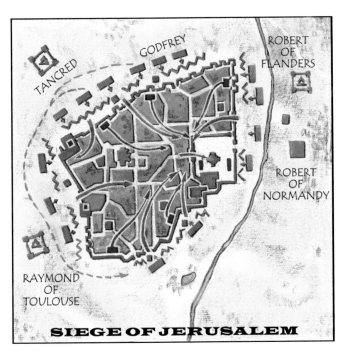

SIEGE OF JERUSALEM

Bohemond wanted the principality for his own. It did not help that the papal legate, Adhemar, who could have overruled any opinion, died on August 1 of an epidemic that ravaged Antioch after the Turkish defeat. An invitation was sent to the pope to assume primacy over all retaken lands. Distance, of course, precluded immediate papal response.

As the nobles squabbled, the rabble they led grew impatient and threatened to raze Antioch if no move was made on Jerusalem. The poorest soldiers protested the loudest. To occupy their time the raiding parties were sent deep into Turkish territory to find supplies and kill more enemies. The strategically important town of Ma'arat-an-Numan, 60 miles southeast of Antioch, was captured in December after a two-week siege by rival groups from Bohemond and Raymond's camps. In the captured city, all the men were slaughtered and the women and children enslaved. As at Antioch, the occupiers soon ran out of food and many resorted to cannibalism, eating the more tender parts of the Turks they had killed. Again, the poorest crusaders grumbled and began to tear down Ma'arat's walls to deny their nobles any comforts and to persuade them to move on to Jerusalem.

On January 13, 1099, a barefoot Raymond of Toulouse, the tired old warrior, led a ragged army of fifteen thousand on the road to Jerusalem, reluctantly leaving Bohemond to rule Antioch as its first Christian prince. It had been almost six months since Kerbogha had been driven away. With Raymond went Tancred and Godfrey of Bouillon. Bohemond and Baldwin, who now possessed princedoms of their own, remained to tend their new realms.

Jerusalem had been recaptured from the Seljuk Turks by the Fatimid caliph in Cairo in 1098, while the Christians besieged Antioch. After Kerbogha's defeat, envoys from Cairo had been sent to the crusader leaders, guaranteeing safety and unfettered access to all holy places for all Christian pilgrims if they did not attack Jerusalem. The offer was rejected. Meanwhile, the Byzantine emperor, though promising to join the crusaders in June, was at the same time negotiating a neutral policy with the Fatimid caliph.

It took another six months to reach Jerusalem. Although local emirs by now had heard of the crusaders' prowess and ruthlessness and were opening their gates and offering alliances, Raymond decided to attack the strategic town of Arqah to put additional pressure on the emir of Tripoli to offer up more of his wealth. After three frustrating months, Raymond had to admit defeat and continue on to Jerusalem. During this futile siege, French knights began to openly accuse the finder of the Holy Lance, Peter Bartholomew, as a fraud and charlatan. The peasant celebrity offered to walk through fire to prove the veracity of his "visions" and died of his burns after a few days.

The Christian army finally saw the Mount of Olives and the domes of Jerusalem on June 7, 1099. Jerusalem was even then an impressive sight, surrounded by a main curtain wall forty to fifty feet high and a lower outer wall. The golden Dome of the Rock, where Abraham went to offer his son as sacrifice and from where the prophet Muhammad rose to heaven, dominated its skyline. A ditch surrounded the city, and a moat encircled its citadel, the Tower of David. At the sight of the holy places, many crusaders wept and prayed. Then they began the siege.

General Iftikhar-al-Daula and his Egyptian garrison prepared for the arrival of the Franks by expelling all Christians, harvesting crops, and poisoning the wells outside the city. Reinforcements had been called from Cairo. Again bereft of siege engines, the crusaders nevertheless launched their first assault. After six days of fighting, the crusader attack was repulsed. With potable water scarce and no victory in sight, many crusaders now wanted to give up and go home.

Despite being engaged in battle, rivalries for supremacy among the remaining leaders of the crusade continued unchecked. Tancred, who had sworn allegiance to Raymond, now switched to Godfrey's banner. Again, religious visions played a great part in their fortunes. A priest named Peter Desiderius claimed to have spoken with the spirit of the dead papal legate, Adhemar of Le Puy, who counseled each to turn from sin, to fast, and to walk around the city's walls in bare feet. If these were done, victory would be attained in nine days.

And so, with priests carrying relics, such as the Holy Lance of Antioch and the arm bone of St. George, the ragged host of hardly fifteen thousand men and women circled Jerusalem in a solemn procession while taunted by their Muslim enemies. The penitential rite culminated at the Mount of Olives where Peter the Hermit and other clerics gave impassioned sermons to lift the army's flagging spirits.

With the crusader army now imbued with religious zeal, all that was needed was wood to build siege equipment to ensure victory over the heretics. During a foraging mission, Tancred discovered some ship's timbers in a cave. Then, six Genoese and English ships reached Jaffa by way of Byzantium to deliver supplies. Two ships were beached and dismantled to provide wood for siege engines. Two huge siege towers were built, along with a battering ram and catapults.

On July 14, the final assault began as Raymond of Toulouse filled in the moat in front of the southern Zion Gate. Godfrey with Tancred and Robert of Normandy demolished the outer wall at the northern Herod's Gate using a battering ram protected by an overhead roof of shields and skins. As the siege towers were rolled to the walls, the defenders responded with a mighty barrage of stones, arrows, and Greek fire, a highly flammable viscous mixture of resin and sulfur. Each time the towers and siege engines caught fire, water and vinegar extinguished the flames. The battle raged all day and throughout the night.

On the morning of July 15, Godfrey's men were able to move their siege tower to the wall and leap onto the ramparts with Tancred in the lead. Hundreds of men followed him into the city. Egyptian troops guarding the southern wall saw the breakout on the northern side and abandoned their posts, allowing Raymond and his men to scale the walls and chase the Muslim soldiers to the citadel where the Egyptian commander surrendered. Jerusalem had fallen.

Throughout the city crusaders slaughtered any non-crusader they met. Large numbers of Muslims seeking refuge in the temple were massacred. Jews who escaped to their synagogue were burned alive. The Christians went from house to house killing and looting. Bellies were slit open to look for swallowed coins. Hands, heads and various body parts filled the streets. The knights tripped over corpses as they hauled their booty. Oddly, in the midst of this bloodlust, there was no rape.

Greek Orthodox Christians were harassed into surrendering a piece of the "True Cross," a piece of timber that would be a rallying point and inspiration for the Franks for many years. When they had their fill, the conquerors gathered at the Holy Sepulcher to offer thanks and penitence to God. Jerusalem was Christian once again.

Pope Urban II died a few days before word of the triumph reached Rome. The Frankish occupiers now chose Godfrey as the compromise choice to rule the city. Disdaining the title of king, he was to rule Jerusalem for a year before dying suddenly of illness or poisoning.

The First Crusade was the only truly successful crusade for the Christians. The military accomplishment can only be considered miraculous. In spite of a divided leadership that distrusted one another as much as they did the enemy, a polyglot army that spoke at least four languages, no organized system of logistics, thousands of miles from home, and traveling mostly on foot through uncharted deserts and over trackless crags in extremes of weather, the crusaders had vanquished the larger armies of a war-tested adversary defending its own territory.

Victory was achieved in the face of such odds only because the timing of their arrival was exquisitely perfect. Their invasion occurred just as the Seljuks were being driven away by their subjugated co-religionists. The crusaders came when the centers of power in the Arab world—Baghdad, Cairo, Damascus, and Aleppo—were rivals in their own struggles for primacy. The Saracen kingdoms could not coordinate their resistance to the infidels because neighboring emirates were engaged

Frankish cavalry drive away Seljuk relief forces outside Antioch on February 9, 1098.

in fighting each other. In less than a century, all this would change. Charismatic leaders would rise, each in turn using the presence of Christian interlopers in their midst to unite the Muslim world. The imams and poets of Cairo, Damascus, and Baghdad would write poems, songs, and sermons lamenting Jerusalem's loss to the cruel infidels. From this fertile soil of victimhood would rise militant Islam.

Above: The First Crusade was the only truly successful crusade. The accomplishment can only be considered miraculous. Picture to left: Tancred leads the final assault on Jerusalem's walls.

"As many of the tired veterans of the crusade left for home, new groups of pilgrims left Europe in 1100 upon hearing the victorious tidings from the Middle East."

After Raymond and Godfrey together repulsed a large Egyptian relieving army at Ascalon, the Europeans settled into their new conquests. Many crusaders went home, having fulfilled their pilgrim vow, leaving Palestine to be held with fewer than one thousand knights. Godfrey now ruled the Kingdom of Jerusalem, which started north of Beirut and ended in Gaza. Bohemond was Prince of Antioch; Baldwin was the ruler of Edessa. Raymond of Toulouse established the principality of Tripoli, north of the Kingdom of Jerusalem and south of Antioch in what is now North Lebanon. Tancred was granted a fiefdom in Galilee. The Latin East or the Outremer, as the Christian conquest would be called, appeared on the map to be a contiguous land stretching from north of the Taurus Mountains, northeast to the Euphrates, and south to Gaza. The vow made to the Byzantine Emperor Alexius to yield control of conquered lands was quietly forgotten. The Franks would keep their new principalities.

In 1099 Bohemond of Antioch traveled to Jerusalem to worship and celebrate Christmas in the Holy City. Instead he was ambushed by a Turkish emir and subsequently imprisoned in a castle dungeon at Niksar in Anatolia. Tancred gave up Galilee to take over Antioch in the absence of the captive Bohemond.

As many of the tired veterans of the crusade left for home, new groups of pilgrims left Europe in 1100 upon hearing the victorious tidings from the Middle East. Large contingents from France, Italy, and Germany reached Constantinople in the spring. Many of the new arrivals had heard of Bohemond's capture and had vowed to liberate this great hero of the First Crusade. Raymond of Toulouse, who happened to be in Constantinople, agreed to aid in the rescue of Bohemond. These new armies traveled separately, divided along ethnic lines and choosing not to form a larger, more powerful joint host, and each in turn was defeated by the Turks before they reached the Taurus Mountains. Though Raymond survived to return to Tripoli, and a few reached Jerusalem, most died or were enslaved. Nobles, such as Hugh of Vermandois and the famous deserter Stephen of Blois, who had returned home in 1098 prior to Jerusalem's capture, lost their lives in this futile attempt to rescue their soiled reputations.

Installing themselves into newly acquired territories, the crusader conquerors now established the mechanisms of colonization. Pilgrims arriving from Europe were welcomed as settlers and new draftees. The crusader rulers occupied their time in the first fifteen years of their rule with creating laws to govern their new subjects, establishing economies and taxation, as well as protecting their acquired realms with new armies and fortifications. As time passed, their Arab adversaries became neighbors, and a hybrid European–Levantine culture evolved mixing Christian rule with an Arabic lifestyle. It was not rare to find Franks wearing turbans and Saracen robes, partaking of local dishes and drink and frequenting baths as any citizen of these lands would. Within the towns and cities a degree of toleration was practiced on both

Above: Newly arrived German knight.
Picture to right: Battle of Ascalon..

Above: A year after the fall of Jerusalem, a rearguard force of Christians was massacred in Anatolia.
Picture to right: Heavy cavalry charges by the Frankish knights easily dispersed the lightly armored Muslim horsemen.

sides. Outside the walls, the Christians fought an endless string of battles against various emirates.

The principalities of Edessa and Tripoli were vassals to the king of Jerusalem. Godfrey annexed as many as twenty Muslim towns and assessed taxes on the emirs of Caesarea, Acre, and Ascalon. Many of these would eventually rise in revolt.

Upon Godfrey's death in 1100, Baldwin came from Edessa to assume the crown of Jerusalem. Baldwin would rule for 18 years. His last few years were marked with increased armed conflict with his Muslim subjects and natural disasters such as drought, locusts, and famine throughout the crusader states. On his deathbed he chose his cousin, Baldwin of Bourg, as his successor. As Baldwin II (1118–1131), his reign would face even greater challenges than his predecessor's.

Soon jihad would be preached throughout the Muslim world, as a means of uniting the fractured Islamic states. In 1119, Ilghazi, the Turkish emir of Aleppo, joined armies with the emir of Damascus and marched on Antioch. Tancred's nephew, Roger, who then ruled Antioch, disregarded Baldwin's command

to wait for him and his army of the kingdom of Jerusalem. Roger's impatience resulted in his death, along with the massacre of his outnumbered army on their way to Aleppo.

Ilghazi's Muslim army did not follow up this victory with further attacks on the Latin principalities. Ilghazi returned to Aleppo a hero. However, he failed to sustain the fervor that could have driven the Franks out of the conquered lands. Instead, in the three years following his success at Aleppo, he slowly drank himself to death.

Ilghazi's nephew, Balak, took up the mantle of jihad with as much initial success as his uncle, first capturing Joscelin, King Baldwin's cousin, then King Baldwin himself. He began a campaign to reconquer the northern region. Among the Franks, his very name brought hopeless dread. He may likely have been the one to unite the Muslim world in jihad, but his career was cut short by an arrow during the siege of a Christian castle.

With the death of Balak, the Latin principalities recovered their power, while the Muslim world

The Turks exacted revenge on the rearguard columns for their defeat at Dorylaeum.

returned to its customary rivalries and feuds. It would take three more generations of charismatic leaders before Jerusalem could be recovered.

Zengi: The First Uniter

Imad ad-Din Zengi, a Turk, was made the governor of Mosul by the Seljuk sultan of Baghdad in 1126. With the sultan's blessing, he took over Aleppo where he began to build a powerful army. In 1131, Fulk of Anjou succeeded his father-in-law, Baldwin II, as the king of Jerusalem. Zengi ambushed Fulk and his bodyguard capturing them in a castle near Tripoli. Fulk was released, upon his promise to pay a ransom. This capture and ransom earned Zengi great fame and a considerable following.

When Zengi set his sights on Damascus, the suspicious Damascenes turned to the king of Jerusalem for help, and facing the odd alliance of Christian and Muslim armies, Zengi retreated.

In 1144, Zengi took advantage of Fulk's death and a feud between Joscelin of Edessa and Raymond of Antioch. He captured Edessa by luring its army out of the city, then besieging its weakly defended walls. After a month his miners toppled the city's wall and on Christmas Eve entered Edessa. He allowed an initial frenzy of slaughter, then magnanimously ended it after the Frankish men were slain, sparing native Christians and the non-Roman Catholic churches.

Edessa's fall was hailed throughout the Muslim world. Zengi was now proclaimed the great victor and glorious uniter who would lead Muslims to the reconquest of the rest of the Latin kingdoms and return Jerusalem to Muslim hands. Jihad had finally found its champion.

Alas, two years later, a drunken Zengi died at the hands of his own eunuch who feared punishment for

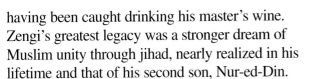

having been caught drinking his master's wine. Zengi's greatest legacy was a stronger dream of Muslim unity through jihad, nearly realized in his lifetime and that of his second son, Nur-ed-Din.

Nur-ed-Din, the Light of Religion

Nur-ed-Din was the quintessential devout Muslim, a Taliban for his time. Unlike his alcoholic father, he forswore drink and banned wine from his camp. He forbade music and ordered tambourines, flutes, and other musical instruments destroyed as objects displeasing to God. He fought Christians and Shi'ite Muslims alike, expelling his schismatic brethren from Aleppo and other cities he came to control. Sunni religious leaders revered him, and through them the message of jihad and unity with Nur-ed-Din as its beacon was propagated.

Just as Nur-ed-Din was taking over his father's emirate at Aleppo, Joscelin successfully reclaimed his old city of Edessa. Nur-ed-Din acted swiftly and recovered the gem of his father's career. This so impressed the Muslim world that even the governor of Damascus who was still allied to the Franks offered his daughter's hand in marriage.

Nur-ed-Din was now hailed as the next uniter, the new leader of jihad.

Pilgrims being escorted by Frankish knights. The Knights Templar came into being, safeguarding pilgrims as they traveled to and from Jerusalem.

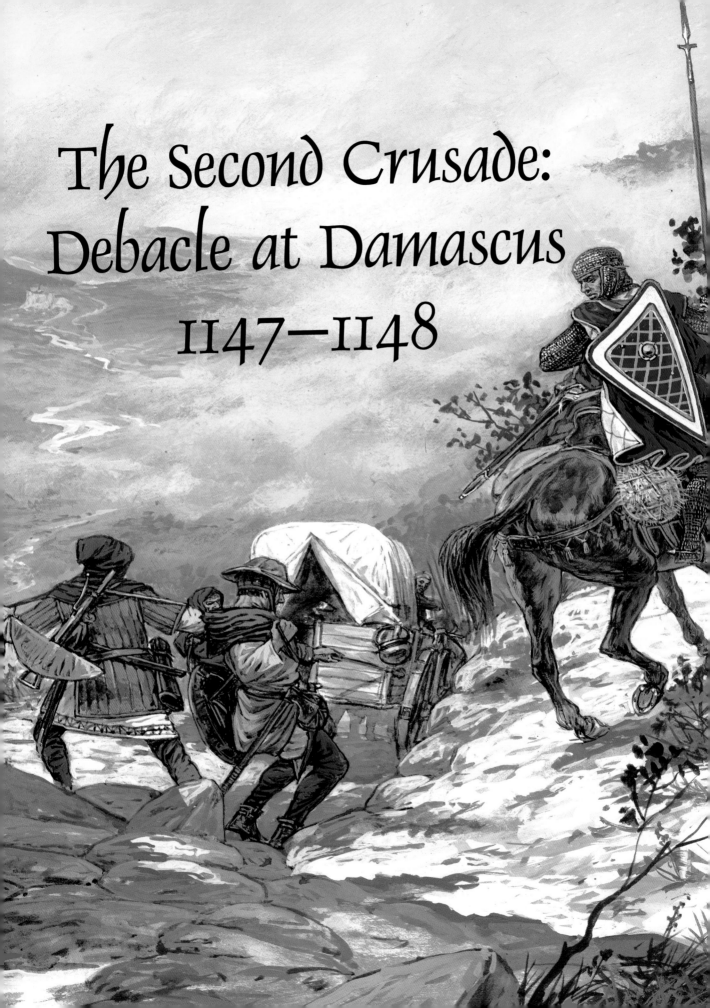

The Second Crusade: Debacle at Damascus 1147–1148

> *"The confused Christian commanders decided to withdraw. A humiliating retreat where many knights were killed by mounted archers marked the ignominious end of the Second Crusade."*

Christianity, and the crusader's vow as expiation for one's sins, past and future. He personally shamed the Holy Roman Emperor, Conrad III (1138–1152), into taking the cross and leading an army to the Middle East. The French king, Louis VII (1137–1180), did not need much cajoling, and so followed Conrad's army on the southeastern trek through Constantinople into Anatolia. The armies departed in late spring of 1146.

The Byzantine emperor, Manuel I Comnenus (1143–1180), persuaded Conrad to march onward and not wait for the French contingents. Conrad proceeded into Anatolia guided by Greeks. He divided his expedition, sending the baggage trains, women, and poorly equipped auxiliaries to take the safer coast road, while the men-at-arms followed the more dangerous direct inland route across the Taurus Mountains.

A Turkish-led army under the son of Kilij Arslan ambushed Conrad on the dry plain near Dorylaeum, and the tired and thirsty crusader army was nearly annihilated. Conrad and the remnants of his ranks made their way to the safety of the coast road, cursing the treachery of their Greek guides for leading them into ambush. Conrad returned to Constantinople to recover from illness and exhaustion.

The news of the fall of Edessa was received with great shock and sorrow in the dank castles and candlelit cathedrals of Western Europe, but those who called for another crusade were greeted with disinterest and even disdain. It needed another charismatic orator to fan the dying embers of fanaticism. For this generation, it was Bernard, abbot of Clairvaux.

Already a famous preacher, Bernard seized on the fall of Edessa as God's punishment for wayward

Above: Frankish knights battling Turkish soldiers.
Picture to right: The last stand around the royal standard at Hattin
Picture to left: Conrad's army marches into Anatolia.

Above: The hardships of a foot soldier in Anatolia.
Picture to right: The Battle of the Orchards of Damascus.

Meanwhile, Louis VII's army had crossed the Bosphorus and proceeded down the coast road to Antioch. Louis had won a commitment from the Emperor Manuel for a fleet to pick up his army at Attalia for the final leg to Jerusalem. The Byzantine fleet arrived with too few in ships to accommodate the entire army. Louis loaded his cavalry and his household, leaving the rest of the contingents to travel overland to Antioch. When Louis arrived at Antioch, he was warmly welcomed by Prince Raymond, who was two generations descended from the late Raymond of Toulouse. Raymond saw in the new arrivals the forces he needed to attack Aleppo and to destroy Nur-ed-Din's growing power. Louis was adamant about going to Jerusalem first.

It so happened that accompanying Louis on his crusade was his beautiful, ambitious, and headstrong wife, Eleanor of Aquitaine, a striking beauty in her mid-twenties and niece of Prince Raymond. Eleanor, who was perhaps frustrated by the monkish Louis and his vow to remain celibate until he worshiped in Jerusalem, now began a fevered flirtation with her forty-nine-year-old dashing uncle and was vocal in supporting his plans and deriding her husband's.

Louis prepared for his departure for Jerusalem and sent for his wife, who then announced her desire for a divorce and her intention to stay with her uncle. A midnight abduction of the queen by Louis' men ended the standoff. (This was not the end of Eleanor's crusader link— Richard Plantagenet, otherwise known as the Lionheart, her son by husband Henry II of England, would himself lead a crusade in another forty years.)

The European reinforcements brought a great sense of relief to the Christians of Jerusalem hemmed in by Nur-ed-Din's forces. Conrad, who had sailed separately, Louis, and the now king of Jerusalem, King Baldwin III (1143–1163), conferred a council of war at Acre to plan the coming campaign. The Franks decided on a course of war that even now stupefies any student of the era— instead of Aleppo or Edessa, they would attack their ally, Damascus!

Scarcely five years earlier, Damascus had asked Jerusalem for help in resisting Zengi's advances. Although the fervor of jihad had begun to infect the general population of the city, its rulers still saw the Christians as their trump card against the ambitions of the rulers of Aleppo, Baghdad, or Cairo. Perhaps Bernard's sermons urging the obliteration of the Saracens precluded the practice of *Realpolitik* as a means to achieve the ultimate end. A dead Saracen, even a friendly one, was indeed the only good Saracen. The visitors overruled the locals. They marched on a friendly city.

The combined crusader armies may have numbered as many as fifty thousand. The onslaught that began on May 25, 1148, bogged down in the thicket of orchards that ringed the city walls. After days of confused hand-to-hand combat, the Franks finally controlled the bloody walled paths and hedgerows. A stalemate ensued while Muslim reinforcements made their way to the city. Another questionable decision that resulted in a Christian debacle was made. The Franks withdrew from the relative safety of the orchards and gathered in an open plain, perhaps to give their superior cavalry the advantage of favorable topography and to escape the Saracen raiding parties skulking in the bushes. But on the treeless plain they found themselves distant from water and shelter from Saracen missiles. The Muslims retook the vacated gardens and counterattacked. With the threat of massive Muslim reinforcements on their way and no source of water, the confused Christian commanders decided to withdraw. This humiliating retreat in which many knights were killed by mounted archers marked the ignominious end of the Second Crusade. Suspicion was strong that it had all been a sellout by the local barons to preserve the alliance with Damascus.

King Louis returned the next year to Europe, full of recriminations and self-doubt. Those that advocated the failed crusade faced tremendous vilification. Even Bernard of Clairvaux was called the anti-Christ.

Meanwhile, Nur-ed-Din consolidated his power in the Saracen world. The fanatical core of his army consisted of Kurds, a Muslim people recently driven from Georgia by a Christian resurgence.

A patient man, he began a diplomatic courtship of the Damascenes in 1150, while his army surrounded their city. He did this four times in four years without attacking and in spite of the city leaders' vow to call

The Assassins (Hashishyyin)

After the prophet Mohammed's death, Islam split into the mainstream Sunni and the schismatic Shia factions. The Shi'ites believed that authority lay with the descendants of Fatima, the prophet's daughter, and her husband, Ali. A descendant of the Fatimid line would someday become the Mahdi, the righteous one who would bring justice and power. A century later the Shi'ites produced another splinter group, the Ismailis, in a dispute over whose family would produce the Mahdi. The Ismailis founded the powerful Fatimid caliphate of Egypt, whose power extended to Sicily and Tunisia.

In the eleventh century, Hassan as-Sabah, a fanatical Persian Ismaili convert, began a campaign of terror against his religious adversaries. From a mountain castle in Persia called Alamut, he trained a small elite force of killers. They were called Hashishyyin by their enemies from the common belief that they were under the influence of hashish when carrying out their deadly duties. Their favored method was a quick thrust of a dagger blessed by the Grand Master and an almost magical disappearance. The Assassins were masters of disguise and provoked fear at their mere mention. Hassan died in 1124, leaving a cadre of dedicated killers whose victims included a Persian grand vizier, a Fatimid caliph and even the caliph of Baghdad. A second group established a base in the Syrian mountains south of

Antioch in 1135. Their leader, Sinan ibn Salman, became known as the "Old Man of the Mountains." His victims now included crusaders, but Sunni leaders were still high on his list, including Saladin who toppled the Shi'ite Fatimid caliphate in Cairo. After two failed attempts at killing Saladin, Sinan decided to spare him but left as a warning a poisoned dagger by his head while he slept. Saladin did not attack the Assassins again.

The Assassins slew Count Raymond II of Tripoli in 1152, but the most notable Assassin murder was that of Conrad of Montferrat, newly anointed king of Jerusalem, in 1192. Richard the Lionheart was suspected of making the arrangements to place his own man, Henry of Champagne, on the throne.

Henry of Champagne did visit Sinan's successor in his stronghold a few years after Conrad's death and witnessed an impressive demonstration of the assassins' blind obedience. The Grand Master barked an order, and two of his soldiers dutifully ran to the ramparts and jumped to their deaths.

The Mongols destroyed the Persian base of the Assassins in 1257 on their way to Baghdad. A few years later the Mamluk sultan, Baybars, shattered the Syrian wing.

on the Franks for help (which lends credence to the suspicion that the debacle at Damascus was a sellout of the visiting Europeans by their Outremer brothers who did not want to attack Damascus in the first place). Damascus finally opened its gates to Nur-ed-Din without a struggle in April 1154. The consolidation of Muslim Syria was now complete.

Egypt also fell within Nur-ed-Din's hegemony, but it took fifteen more years, and less peacefully than did Damascus. The Fatimid caliph in Cairo was merely a figurehead at this time. The vizier, whom he appointed or was forced to appoint with the consent of various factions, exercised the real power. In 1163, the position of vizier had little longevity in office. Offend one faction and he was dead. An ex-vizier named Shawar, who survived his loss of office, turned to Nur-ed-Din for help in regaining his ministry— offering lands, gold, and one-third of Egypt's grain revenues as incentive. Nur-ed-Din sent an army under his most trusted general, Shirkuh, a one-eyed rotund Kurd, who had a young nephew named Saladin who acted as his second-in-command. The usurper was easily ousted.

However, Shawar, upon regaining his seat, refused to recognize his debt to Nur-ed-Din, even calling on Jerusalem's Franks under Amalric (1163–1174), Baldwin III's son and successor, to assist him in sending home Shirkuh and his soldiers. Shirkuh withdrew after a three-month standoff with the combined Fatimid–Frank army.

Two years later Nur-ed-Din sent Shirkuh and Saladin back to Egypt, and they were again defeated by Amalric's Franks and Shawar's Fatimids. Curiously, in 1168, Amalric attacked and massacred the inhabitants of Bilbeis, a Fatimid town, possibly suspecting collusion between Shawar and Nur-ed-Din. Shawar, even more curiously, invited his enemies, Shirkuh and Saladin, into Cairo to help defend him against his former Frankish allies. In 1169, Shirkuh entered Cairo and deposed Shawar who was then personally beheaded by Saladin. Thus, the centuries-old Fatimid empire came under Nur-ed-Din's hegemony, which now covered the contiguous lands from northern Iraq to Egypt. Shirkuh now became vizier of Egypt, but died within a month. Saladin naturally replaced his uncle.

Louis VII of France (1120–1180)

Louis VII was the son of Louis le Gros (the Fat, Louis VI), a man of great appetite and greed. Far different from his father, the son was a pious and gentle man who preferred a simple life of learning and prayer. He took over the crown upon his father's death in 1137.

His assertion of royal rights over Toulouse brought him to a painful struggle with Pope Innocent II who had appointed his own nephew as that city's bishop. Louis chased the new bishop out of Toulouse and pursued him to Vitry where he burned the cathedral, trapping three hundred souls sheltering within. Appalled at the loss of life, he asked the pope's forgiveness and embarked on the Second Crusade as a means of expiation. He took along his powerful first wife, Eleanor of Aquitaine.

After the fiasco at Damascus, he returned to France a dispirited man. He married three times, divorcing each previous wife for her inability to produce a male heir. His third wife, Alice of Champagne, finally bore him a son in 1167, Philip Augustus, who would become one of France's greatest kings.

Louis was just and quite tolerant for his era, extending protection to all Jews in France. He accomplished a consolidation of royal power, with the Ile de France as his power base. His greatest challenge emerged when Henry Plantagenet, who would become Henry II of England, married Louis' former wife, Eleanor of Aquitaine, thereby creating a large rebellious suzerainty composed of Eleanor's duchy of Aquitaine and Henry's fiefs of Normandy and Anjou. It would be left to Louis' son Philip to assert French authority over these Plantagenet areas.

Eleanor of Aquitaine (1122–1204)

She is simply the most fascinating woman in the history of the Middle Ages. She was the daughter of William IX, the last duke of Aquitaine and Aenor, viscountess of Châtellerault. Her given name was "Alia Aenor" in Latin, "the other Aenor" which was shortened to Eleanor.

She succeeded her father as ruler of the duchy in 1138, the same year she was married to then Prince Louis of France. The marriage was a mismatch between a monkish recluse and a beautiful, free-spirited, headstrong woman. They became estranged during the Second Crusade and were divorced upon their return to France in 1152, in spite of a newborn daughter. She quickly married Henry Plantagenet of Anjou who soon became Henry II of England.

She bore Henry eight children through a marriage of thirty-seven years that resembled more of an armed truce between perpetual combatants. Among these progeny were future kings of England— Richard the Lionheart and John Lackland. She was an assertive and controlling queen who often intervened in her husband's affairs of state and flesh. She was devoted to the fine arts; her court at Poitiers was a center of music and an origin of the literary notions of courtly love. Devoted to her sons, especially Richard, she encouraged them to rebel against their father who imprisoned her for ten years.

She helped Richard establish his kingship in 1189 and helped stabilize the realm upon his death in 1199. She spent her last years in the convent at Fontevrault where she was buried next to Richard and Henry.

Above: A soldier of Saladin's army watches the Christians leave Jerusalem.
Picture next page: Sultan Saladin and his personal bodyguard.

The Military Orders

Several powerful organizations evolved from small groups of early crusaders dedicated to the humanitarian needs of pilgrims. These communities became independent religious military elites recognized by the pope, with activities expanding from charity to warfare, and later, to commerce. These orders would establish their own fiefs and later their own states. Strict laws enforced by a rigid hierarchy governed the lives of each member.

Knights Templar

In 1115, two Burgundian knights, Hugues des Payens and Godfroi de St. Omer, with a single horse between them, founded "The Order of the Poor Knights of Christ," dedicated to protection of pilgrims in the Holy Land. They escorted vulnerable groups of pilgrims to Palestine. King Baldwin II of Jerusalem granted them space in a building on the site of Solomon's Temple, from which came their name—Knights of the Temple of Solomon or Templars for short. By 1124, their ranks had grown, and the community became an official order of soldier-monks under the strict rules of the Cistercian Order. The religious vows of chastity, poverty, and obedience were strictly enforced. The military vows of defending Jerusalem to the death and refusal to give quarter to Muslims were enthusiastically observed. The core of the order were the knights who wore a small red Latin cross on white cloaks. Sergeants and chaplains made up the supporting ranks. They were fierce warriors, known for their discipline and battlefield prowess. They inspired fear among the Muslims who respected their willingness to die fighting.

The order was lavished with gifts of property and money and soon established communities in Europe. Its wealth necessitated the creation of a financial system to manage the transfer of funds from one priory to another. The Templars became the pre-eminent bankers of their day, serving not only their own, but much of Europe's commercial needs.

King Philip of France, jealous of the power and wary of the secrecy of the order, arrested, tortured, and executed most of the order's members in his country in 1307. Their assets were acquired by the French and English monarchs, and by 1312, the Templars were officially suppressed by the pope.

The Hospitallers of St. John of Jerusalem

In 1113, a certain Brother Gerard of the Augustine Order aquired a hospice named after St. John the Baptist to care for the sick of Jerusalem. Godfrey of Bouillon had granted the brothers some land for their charitable works. As more donations poured in, the order extended its humanitarian reach to Italy and France. In 1120, the pope recognized the Hospitallers as an independent order. With the charter came the right to defend their hospitals throughout the Holy Land. This led to the creation of a military arm.

The Grand Commander governed the two arms of the order—the men and women of the Hospitallers and the military contingents of knights and sergeants. The order acquired several castles of which the majestic Krak des Chevaliers in Syria was the greatest. It was the crowning achievement of Outremer castle design. The order's European establishment was extensive, organized into seven sectors called langues (tongues), subdivided into provinces, priories, and commanderies. It was inevitable that the Hospitallers would come into conflict with the Templars, with whom they competed for control of towns and commercial opportunity. These religious orders fought each other in the streets of Acre in the mid-1200s. The Hospitallers lost Acre, their last stronghold, in 1291 and moved to Cyprus. There they became a naval force, eventually capturing Rhodes from the Saracens in 1309. They prospered for two centuries, renaming themselves the Knights of Rhodes. Chased out by the Turks, they reestablished themselves as the Knights of Malta in 1522.

The Hospitallers adopted a black mantle with a small white cross as their heraldry. Their shields were black overlaid with a white cross.

The Teutonic Knights

This order started as a single hospital for German crusaders in the 1140s under the aegis of the Hospitallers. After Saladin shut it down in 1187, a new hospital was established in Acre after that city's recapture by Richard the Lionheart in 1190. From there the Teutonic Knights rapidly grew to be an independent order patterned after the Templars and Hospitallers, governed by a hochmeister (Grand Master). It received Pope Innocent III's recognition in 1196, being given the heraldry of a white habit adorned with a black cross. The order would never attain the stature of the Templars and Hospitallers in Palestine. In 1229, the order left the Holy Land to concentrate on the conversion of pagan tribes in the Baltic region. Over the next two centuries, from their East Prussian headquarters of Marienburg, they became the dominant power in that area until their defeat at the hands of a combined Polish-Lithuanian army at Grunwald in 1410. The order's power faded from then on, becoming vassals of the ascendant Polish kingdom in 1467, and becoming secularized when the hochmeister, Albrecht von Brandenburg, converted to Lutheranism in 1525. They have been immortalized in national histories of their adversaries for the ignominious defeats they suffered, notably, at Grunwald and earlier in 1242 at Lake Peipus, at the hands of Alexander Nevsky's Russian army of Novgorod. The rise of German nationalism in the nineteenth and twentieth centuries used the Christian militarism of the Teutonic Order as a source of inspiration.

The Third Crusade:
The Loss of Jerusalem
1189—1192

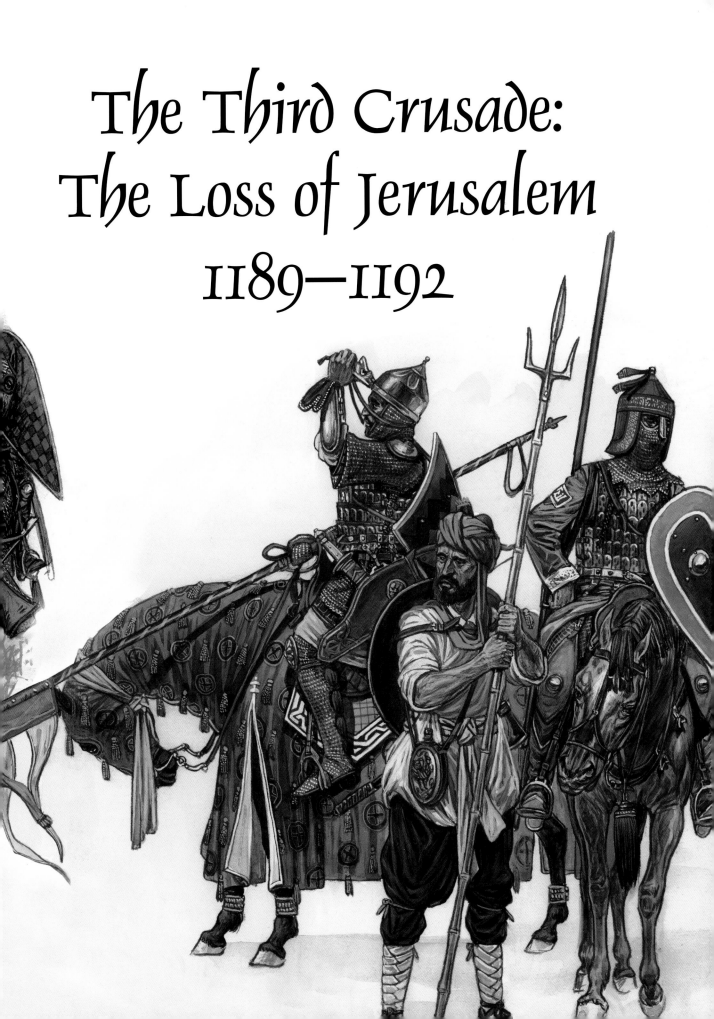

> *"Richard sallied forth on an old inferior horse to challenge the Saracens to individual combat. Saladin sent a majestic charger to Richard with his compliments, remarking that Richard deserved a better mount."*

As vizier of Egypt, Saladin was required to consult with and obey the edicts of Nur-ed-Din. In a few years, it became apparent that the young Kurd Saladin had become too wealthy and popular in his Egyptian fiefdom for Nur-ed-Din's taste, with power rivaling his master. Nur-ed-Din suspected that Saladin was withholding tribute and began to refer to him as "the Upstart." Saladin continued to play the obsequious lackey, publicly showing respect and deference to Nur-ed-din, but making his own decisions to Nur-ed-Din's frustration.

The Rise of Saladin

In 1174, Nur-ed-Din died of natural causes, apparently in the midst of preparing to invade Egypt to depose Saladin. The elders of Damascus chose Saladin to succeed Nur-ed-Din, forcing Nur-ed-Din's eleven-year-old son, al-Salih, to flee. For the next ten years, Saladin had to fight fellow Muslims to consolidate his power. His enemies still saw him as a peasant usurper and supported al-Salih. The caliph of Baghdad, the nominal power in the Islamic world, chose to remain silent about Saladin's legitimacy. In time, Saladin vanquished his adversaries, al-Salih died, and all his efforts then turned to jihad and the recapture of Jerusalem and the Frankish principalities. He had total control over Nur-ed-Din's realm. As the founder of the Ayyubid Dynasty (named after his father, Ayyub), he had no rival.

The Fractious Franks: Christians Divided

Amalric's son, Baldwin IV (1174–1185), contracted leprosy as a child. When Amalric died in the same year as Nur-ed-Din, a thicket of rivalries and conspiracies grew around the expected demise of the thirteen-year-old leper king. Just as the first crusaders captured Jerusalem at a moment of Islamic disunity, the widening rifts in Christian Outremer would deliver Jerusalem back to Islam.

There had always been rivalry among the crusader cities. Antioch and Tripoli bore Jerusalem's overlordship with gritted teeth. With the death of the king of Jerusalem, Amalric IV, the rivalry and power struggles between cities escalated to include power struggles between groups within the cities, further weakening crusader states' unity.

The year 1174 was also the year Amalric's son Baldwin was crowned king. In spite of his devastating illness, Baldwin proved to be an able ruler, negotiating truces with Saladin while he tried to unite and consolidate Christian power. Baldwin's infirmity required that a regent be appointed to assist him in governance. The first regent appointed was Count Raymond III of Tripoli, an able and intelligent man who brought to Baldwin's court many of his own political agendas.

The other major influence on the young king was Guy of Lusignan who was married to the king's sister, Sibylla. As the king's medical condition continued to deteriorate, the various factions in the king's court became emboldened in creating disunity. The king's mother, Agnes de Courtnay, maneuvered Guy of Lusignan into the role of the king's adviser, but the native-born barons supported Raymond, and soon Guy was fired and Count Raymond was back in power. The truce with Saladin was repeatedly broken by the rogue baron of Transjordan, Reynald of Chatillon, a rapacious man in his fifties who was once a prince of Antioch and despoiler of Cyprus in 1156. He had spent sixteen years in Nur-ed-Din's jail and upon his release, acquired his new fiefdom by marriage. Reynald attacked the rich caravans that maintained Muslim commerce and audaciously built a fleet that raided maritime traffic on the Red Sea and even attempted a seaborne attack on Mecca. Saladin vowed to personally kill Reynald.

In March 1185, Baldwin, the leper king, died. His dying wish that his sister Sibylla's seven-year-old son be crowned as Baldwin V, with Raymond of Tripoli staying on as regent was honored. Another truce was made with Saladin, but soon the boy king died. His mother successfully claimed the throne as queen and crowned her husband, Guy of Lusignan, king of Jerusalem. Her rival, Raymond of Tripoli, was thus isolated along with his circle of resentful northern seigneurs.

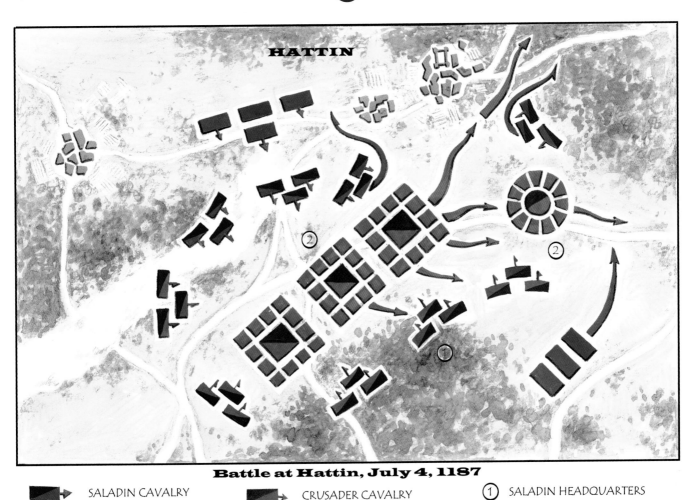

Battle at Hattin, July 4, 1187

◼️➤ SALADIN CAVALRY	◼️➤ CRUSADER CAVALRY	① SALADIN HEADQUARTERS
◼️➤ SALADIN INFANTRY	◼️➤ CRUSADER INFANTRY	② GUY LUSIGNAN HEADQUARTERS

Meanwhile, Reynald of Chatillon attacked another caravan, and Saladin found the time ripe to attack the Christians.

The Battle of Hattin

Saladin began his campaign with an incursion into Galilee, Raymond's fiefdom. A first encounter ended with the death of the Master of the Hospitallers and the Marshal of the Templars. Raymond had no choice but to join the royal army mobilizing at nearby Saffuriyeh. Saladin crossed the Jordan valley to besiege Tiberias on June 30, 1187, trapping Raymond's wife along with the town's small garrison.

King Guy and the rest of the Christian leaders held a council of war fifteen miles away. Raymond, the native warrior, advised against moving on Tiberias,

warning that the heat and the lack of water would only weaken the army further in the face of an enemy that outnumbered them by several thousand. Better to make Saladin come to them. However, the new Master of the Templars accused Raymond of cowardice and sympathy with the Saracens, and on July 3, the Christian army, possibly twenty thousand strong, began the sweltering trek to the western shore of the Sea of Galilee.

They were harassed by mounted archers who rained arrows, then wheeled away before the parched crusaders could retaliate. The dehydrated army rested for the night in the shadow of two hills, the Horns of Hattin, at the foot of which waited Saladin's army.

In the morning, the Saracens added to the Christian army's suffering and thirst by setting grass afire, keeping them from the nearest water a few miles away. The rain of arrows forced many Christian warriors to rush up the slopes of Hattin where they surrendered after beating back several Saracen attacks from below. Raymond escaped with a few knights by riding down his own infantry and slashing through the Muslim lines. King Guy was captured on Hattin along with the raider, Reynald of Chatillon. Saladin kept his vow and personally beheaded the old pirate while sparing Guy.

Jerusalem Recaptured by Islam

After Acre, Beirut, and Jaffa fell in the next month, Saladin prepared to attack Jerusalem. After a thirteen-day siege, the city surrendered. Saladin did not unleash a bloodbath as the Christians had done eighty-eight years before. He imposed a ransom for its Christian inhabitants. Those who could not afford to pay would be enslaved. The number proved large, and Saladin in his mercy released most of them, even giving financial assistance to widows and orphans.

Saladin restored the Muslim shrines that had been converted into Christian quarters, but preserved the Church of the Holy Sepulcher and other Christian churches against the wishes of his retinue. These he turned over to Greek Orthodox control. He allowed pilgrims of all faiths to visit the Holy City.

The reconquest was complete except for the coastal pockets of Tyre, Tripoli, and Antioch. An adventurer named Conrad of Montferrat, arriving just as Tyre had agreed to surrender to Saladin, took over and continued to resist the Saracen besiegers.

Saladin realized that soon his war-weary levies would return home for the winter. To temporarily neutralize these remaining strongholds, he decided to rekindle the old Christian rivalries and feuds. To this end, he released Guy of Lusignan.

Guy predictably broke his vow of peace with Saladin and attempted to reconstitute his court at Tyre. Conrad of Montferrat did not even open the gates for him. So with his dwindled entourage, he proceeded to Acre and began to besiege it, gaining strength as survivors of Hattin and the various fallen strongholds gathered beneath his banner.

The War of the Three Kings

Shortly after hearing the news of Jerusalem's fall, Pope Urban III died—supposedly of despair. His successor, Gregory VIII (1187), issued the call for another crusade. The Holy Roman Emperor, Frederick I Barbarossa (red beard) (1152–1190), a fit warrior at nearly seventy, soon gathered a large army of thirty thousand and began the difficult overland trek to Palestine in May 1189. This army was a disciplined group, not the unruly mobs of the First Crusade.

The traditionally suspicious Byzantine Emperor Isaac Angelus had to be convinced with a German show of force to render assistance. Isaac had great cause for worry because the German army had traveled safely through territory held by rebels. As did previous emperors, he provided the boats for the crossing into Asia Minor.

Frederick's army suffered the usual hunger, thirst, and ambushes in Turkish Anatolia and crossed the Taurus Mountains, much depleted but still with good cohesion. On finally reaching the plains of Christian Cilicia in the heat of the Mediterranean summer, an exuberant Frederick plunged into the Kalycadnus River for a cooling swim and drowned in an eddy.

His death shattered his army. Many went home, some found ships to take them to Antioch and Tripoli, while the greater part walked overland into Syria, many dying along the way. The duke of Swabia, Frederick's son, had his father's body pickled in vinegar to be buried in Jerusalem. The fluid could not

The death of Emperor Frederick I Barbarossa.

prevent the body from decaying in the summer heat, and upon reaching Antioch, Frederick was quickly buried in its cathedral.

Joscius, archbishop of Tyre, had convinced the warring kings, Henry II of England and Philip of France, to call a truce to their border quarrels in Normandy and Aquitaine and raise armies for the Holy Land's rescue. Both kings bided time while raising money through a special tax called the Saladin tithe. In July 1189, Henry's son, Richard (the Lionheart), began a rebellion against his father with Philip's assistance. The humiliated old king died in a few days, leaving Richard his throne.

When Frederick died in June 1190, the English and French kings were still at home in Europe. After a conference in Vezelay, France, the two kings finally departed on July 3, 1190, the third anniversary of the debacle at Hattin. As agreed, the English soldiers wore a white cross, while the French wore a red one, and their Belgian allies a green one. Richard soon parted ways with Philip, planning to meet his fleet at Marseille while Philip's ships awaited him in Genoa.

After settling scores with a usurper in Sicily who had imprisoned his widowed sister, the Sicilian Queen Joan, Richard finally sailed east. Along the way he arranged his marriage to Berengaria, a princess of Navarre, thereby insulting his ally Philip whose sister had been betrothed to him since childhood. A substantial transfer of gold bought Philip's forgiveness.

Storms scattered Richard's fleet in the eastern Mediterranean; some ships, including his sister Joan's, crashed on the Cyprus rocky coast. Cyprus had once been a friendly haven for western crusaders prior to crusader Reynald of Chatillion's brutal invasion in 1156. Chatillion ravaged the island, violated it's nuns, and cut off the noses of its orthodox priests before exiting the island. Since Chatillion's departure visitors did not warrant a warm welcome. Richard defeated the waiting Cypriots and celebrated his conquest by marrying Berengaria.

Philip had already reached Tyre and with his cousin, Lord Conrad of Montferrat, sailed south to Acre. There, the former king of Jerusalem, Guy of Lusignan (1186–1190), had been besieging the coastal city for almost two years. Guy was surrounded by Saladin's soldiers. The besiegers were themselves besieged in a standoff.

Philip reorganized the battle lines around Acre, but dutifully waited for Richard to join in the assault.

Crusader archers and crossbowmen firing at the walls of Acre.

Richard was ill with arnaldia, a rare disease that made his hair and fingernails fall out. When he finally arrived on June 8, 1191, Richard's charismatic leadership infused the Christians with renewed enthusiasm, despite his illness. Within a month, the Turkish garrison capitulated. The victory was achieved in the midst of simmering feuds in the crusader camp. Philip supported his cousin Conrad's claim to Outremer overlordship against Guy's, who was supported by Richard. The Lusignans (under Guy) were Richard's vassals in the English-controlled county of Poitou. The ragged remnants of Frederick's army under Leopold of Austria competed for their share of booty and recognition. Richard would pay dearly for throwing down Leopold's banner from Acre's tower, deeming the Teutonic contribution to the victory to be too miniscule compared to that of the French and English.

Above all this was the aggressive competition between the powerful trading cities of Genoa and Pisa. Each one coveted exclusive trading rights with the rich Middle Eastern principalities, Christian or Muslim, and had fought each other throughout the Mediteranean. Genoa supported Philip and Conrad, Pisa sponsored Richard and Guy.

A deal was struck such that Guy remained king and would hold Acre, while Conrad would continue to be Tyre's lord and would inherit the crown. It was a truce, not a treaty. Philip of France left for home as did Leopold of Austria, both resentful of Richard's primacy. Henceforth, the Third Crusade would be an English-led endeavor. Richard impatiently gathered his English troops and the remaining French, Belgian, and German knights who had decided to stay.

Negotiations with Saladin for a prisoner exchange and the return of the most revered relic, a piece of Christ's True Cross, had broken down. Before departing for Jerusalem on August 22, 1191, Richard proceeded to execute almost three thousand Muslim captives.

The Battle of Arsuf

Richard organized his army's march with sound tactical considerations. His army marched in columns parallel to the shore, with infantry including archers and crossbowmen on the inland flank nearest the shadowing Saracens. Another column of infantry marched parallel to this flank. The innermost column contained the knights and the mounted men-at-arms, and the column nearest the shore was the baggage train. The fleet sailed offshore keeping pace with the soldiers, ready to take on the wounded and to resupply the columns.

Richard began the march in the early morning when the sun was low, with frequent stops near water. The army numbered no more than fourteen thousand, with barely a third on horseback. Richard forbade the breaking of ranks without his explicit order.

Saladin's army, numbering around twenty thousand, consisted mostly of cavalry with a small number of Nubian infantry. Through many days, his mounted bowmen would rain arrows on Richard's columns, thinning the outer ranks and picking off stragglers. Saladin hoped to irritate Richard out of his formations into a disorganized attack, but the Europeans held firm. Even when the Saracens cut off the rearguard comprised of French troops under Hugh, duke of Burgundy, Richard rescued his isolated formation, but still did not order a general attack on Saladin.

After two weeks of harassment, the Christian knights could no longer be held back, pleading with Richard to finally attack. Richard and Saladin, both fighting malaria, scouted for a proper site for the pitched battle, and both identified the same ground.

Saladin positioned his army facing west, with the forest of Arsuf by the marshes of a river covering his right flank on the north, and a row of hills sloping down to the ruins of Arsuf on his left on the south.

On September 7, Richard ordered a slow march toward the Saracens with the express command to keep together and maintain cohesion. Richard's strategy was to have the Muslim horsemen spend their mounts in their typical wheeling attacks and then his men would fall upon their exhausted ranks at the proper time. Saladin wanted to draw the crusaders into the center, turning their left wing in an envelopment screened by the Arsuf forest. The slow pace of the Christian advance frustrated this strategy.

The crusaders struggled to maintain cohesion and continue the slow advance, but vigorous attacks began to collapse the Hospitaller crossbowmen on the right, while the storm of Saracen arrows decimated the mounted horsemen. Still, Richard refused to charge. Fra Garnier of Nablus, the Hospitaller Grand Master, begged for permission to attack and, in frustration, charged the enemy with a few followers without Richard's permission.

Above: Saladin's horsemen goad the crusaders into giving battle.
Picture to left: Crusaders storm Acre's walls.

Richard had no choice but to follow this precipitate assault with the general order to charge, fortuitously catching a good portion of Saladin's army dismounted to better aim their arrows. The fury of the Christian charge drove the Muslims back a mile. As various Saracen contingents reformed to counterattack, Richard skillfully regrouped his cavalry and smashed those formations. Three times he gathered his scattered knights and charged the Muslims. The last frenzied charge put to flight Saladin's personal bodyguard of seven hundred horsemen led by his nephew. The rest of the battered Saracen army finally ran from the battlefield in disarray, pursued by the crusaders.

Arsuf was Richard's masterpiece, a decisive victory that should have ensured Jerusalem's recapture, but Saladin was able to regroup his demoralized warriors quickly and again harass the Christian columns. Richard was forced to divert his army to Jaffa to secure his flank, a delay that doomed the endeavor. As he refortified the city, winter weather arrived, and Richard postponed his advance to Jerusalem.

When Richard resumed the march to Jerusalem at the end of October, Saladin had reinforced the city and ordered an Egyptian army to march to its relief. Richard arrived at Beit Nuba, 12 miles from Jerusalem, within sight of its rooftops on Christmas day. He never came closer. A violent rainstorm and the imminent arrival of the Egyptian force convinced him to return to Jaffa.

Saladin and Richard apparently exchanged messages many times during that winter. Mutual respect grew between them. Richard even proposed a marriage between Saladin's brother, al-Adil, and his sister, Joan, if al-Adil converted to Christianity, and together they would govern Outremer.

During this time, the conspiracies pitting various Christian factions one against another came to full boil. The French and Genoese sailed to capture Acre, while the Pisans rushed to check their move. Although Richard was able to negotiate a shaky peace, he

Battle of Arsuf (1191)

▬	Crusader Infantry
◨	Crusader Cavalry
▻◅	Crusader Convoy
①	Richard the Lionheart
②	Templars
③	Normans
④	Champagnians
⑤	Burgundians
⑥	Hospitallers
◼	Saladin's Defensive Detachment
▬▬	Main forces of Saladin's Army

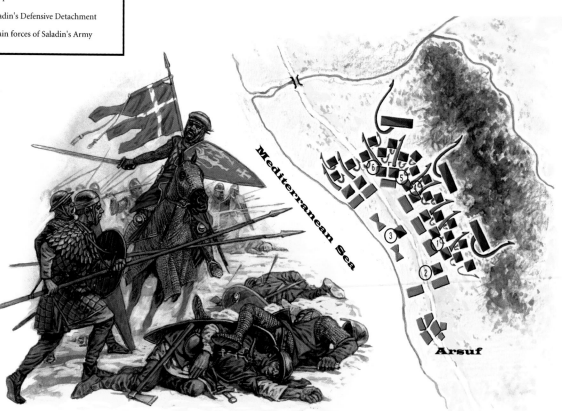

Above: King Richard I supports his infantry at Arsuf. Picture to right: Richard I of England lands his troops at Jaffa.

realized that the conflict had to be resolved by clearly anointing a king. Conrad was chosen by a gathering of Outremer nobles. Richard, knowing that unity in whatever guise was now paramount for Christian survival, abided by this result, mollifying his ally Guy by giving him Cyprus.

More sinister events quickly followed the choice of Conrad. He was killed by Assassins in Tyre before he could be crowned. Suspicion fell on everyone, including Richard, whose faction would have gained the most by Conrad's death. Henry of Champagne replaced Conrad.

The Battle of Jaffa

Richard and Saladin resumed their warfare in the summer of 1192. Richard again marched toward Jerusalem, and at Beit Nuba surprised a rich caravan headed for Jerusalem. Still, Richard was unsure that he had enough forces to prevail, so he returned to Acre.

Saladin prepared for the Christian assault on Jerusalem, but when none materialized, he led his army to besiege Jaffa on August 1. Richard sailed from Acre to Jaffa and found the city under Saracen control. Ever the rash warrior, he jumped into the surf with only half his armor to immediately attack the infidels. He successfully established his camp by the ruined walls; after repelling several attacks, Richard sallied forth on an old inferior horse to challenge the Saracens to individual combat. Saladin sent a majestic charger to Richard with his compliments, remarking that Richard deserved a better mount.

Richard's innovative defensive tactics were prefigurements of methods that would be commonplace in the Renaissance. With two thousand soldiers, he established a defensive perimeter protected from Saracen arrows by palisades (a long fence with pointed stakes). He met Saladin's mounted charges with men armed with long pikes, protected by teams of crossbowmen

situated between every pair. While one fired a crossbow, a second one reloaded another. The few mounted knights available counterattacked any

retreating cavalry. Repeated attacks by the Muslim warriors wilted in the continuous barrage of deadly bolts and the hedgehog of pikes until they refused to obey Saladin's order to advance once more. A lull descended on Jaffa.

When Richard fell ill shortly thereafter, Saladin sent fruit and snow from Mt. Hebron to cool Richard's fever. The impasse at Jaffa was settled the next month with a three-year truce negotiated by the rival monarchs. By the Treaty of Ramleh, Jerusalem would remain in Muslim control, while Christian pilgrims had free and protected access to its holy sites. Saladin agreed to the remaining Christian coastal strongholds from Tyre to Jaffa. And so, many Christian warriors now set off to pray at Jerusalem, but Richard felt unworthy in his failure to recapture God's city, and he left that October for home, never to set foot on the sacred ground of Jerusalem.

The Third Crusade ended in military stalemate. Politically, the landscape was little changed: Jerusalem was still in Muslim hands, and the Christians sat in their coastal fortresses. Richard's fighting skills and assertive leadership had shattered the veneer of invincibility that had been built around Saladin. The great sultan's support began to fray as Richard time and again blunted his moves. The Saracens had grown war-weary, especially their leader. Saladin's rivals, including his brother, had begun to question his authority, and as his hegemony began to fray, Saladin died a tired, sickly warrior of fifty-four, only five short months after Richard's departure. His brother, al-Adil, succeeded him.

Richard returned home worried about Philip's incursions into his French territories and his brother John's ambitions. On the way, he was imprisoned by Leopold, duke of Austria, whose banner he had hurled down from Acre's walls. A huge ransom was paid, and Richard returned to his backyard wars with Philip, dying of an infected wound from a crossbow bolt outside an inconsequential castle he was besieging in France.

King Richard the Lionheart leads the attack at Arsuf.

The Leaders of the Third Crusade

Richard the Lionheart (1157–1199)

Richard I of England has achieved mythical status over the centuries as the embodiment of chivalry, although the reality is that he was one of England's most ineffectual monarchs, leaving his people a legacy of debt for the many wars he fought and the ransom raised when he was imprisoned in Austria. He spoke French and barely knew English. He was indeed a fierce warrior, a keen tactician, and a charismatic leader. At the time of the Third Crusade, he was already, for his era, a middle-aged man in his mid-thirties, but quite striking with his red hair and stocky warrior's physique.

He was the third child of Henry II of England, the first Plantagenet king, and Eleanor of Aquitaine, who made sure that her favorite son was well educated and recognized as the duke of Aquitaine. Henry and Eleanor held more land in France than did the French king, and Henry's refusal to share power with his sons led to civil war, pitting Richard and his older brothers against their father who maintained his iron grip.

Richard was granted Henry's forgiveness and was recognized as his heir in 1183 after the two older sons died, still in rebellion. Henry later withdrew his support for Richard, favoring his youngest son, John. This drove Richard to another rebellion with the help of Philip II Augustus, the new king of France, who would become his mortal enemy. Henry was forced to cede money and power and died shortly thereafter. Richard was crowned king and soon left on his crusade.

Although allies on the crusade, Philip fought the Plantagenets for control of their French possessions of Aquitaine, Anjou, Brittany, Maine, Normandy and Poitou. Philip left Acre for France, leaving Richard to lead the crusade. Philip proceeded to stoke John's ambitions and to attack Richard's French possessions, forcing Richard to negotiate peace with Saladin in order to reclaim his authority at home.

On his way home, Richard was captured by Duke Leopold of Austria, whom Richard had insulted at Acre. He was transferred to Henry VI, the Holy Roman Emperor, and was subsequently ransomed for 100,000 silver marks. Upon his return to England, he had himself recrowned to assert his authority.

He returned to France to wage war against Philip, leaving the governance of his realm to others. He died of a crossbow bolt wound to the neck at Chaluz in France on April 11, 1199. He is buried in the French abbey of Fontevrault next to his parents.

Of all the Christian leaders in all the crusades, Richard possessed the sharpest tactical mind. His logistical organization sustained his forces in a barren land. His grasp of combined arms formations, cavalry with infantry, crossbowmen with spearmen, a fleet sailing offshore for naval support, made him a worthy adversary to Saladin's own military acumen. He even attached a corps of laundrywomen to his army, realizing that cleanliness directly affected the health of his soldiers. In battle, he was a fiery, charismatic leader.

Philip II Augustus (1165–1223)

Philip, a hunchback, is considered France's greatest medieval monarch. His unusually long reign of forty-three years established the supreme power of the crown and greatly expanded royal lands. Born to Louis VII, he of the failed Second Crusade, and his fourth wife, Adele of Champagne. Philip was crowned at fourteen, when Louis suffered from a stroke.

Philip asserted himself early by defeating the combined forces of Flanders, Champagne, and Burgundy, acquiring lands for France. He attacked English territories in 1187, and the next year, allied with Richard, forced Richard's father Henry II to cede part of Anjou to France.

Philip's brief alliances with Richard the Lionheart were born of expedience to gain lands and to ensure his share of glory. He fought with Richard at Acre, but left for home, leaving Richard to mire himself in the Holy Land. He intrigued against Richard in connivance with Prince John during Richard's captivity in Germany. Upon Richard's release, their war restarted, and though he lost the Angevin territories, he outlived his rival and acquired more land by defeating Richard's brother John in 1204. Vast areas that included Anjou, Brittany, Maine, Normandy, and Touraine were taken from the English.

Philip's crowning military achievement was the Battle of Bouvines in 1214 where he defeated the alliance of John of England, the Holy Roman Emperor, Otto IV, and the count of Flanders.

The Leaders of the Third Crusade

His greater legacy was the expansion of France, the creation of an organized civil service to run his realm, the expansion of the judiciary, an efficient tax collection system, and the growth of Paris as a fitting national capital. He built the city walls, the Louvre, paved its streets, oversaw the founding of the University of Paris, and ensured Notre Dame's completion.

Frederick I Barbarossa (1123–1190)

Frederick, an imposing presence, whose red hair and beard earned him his appellation "Barbarossa", is a symbol of German unity to this day. Son of the duke of Swabia and a daughter of the duke of Bavaria, he spent his thirty-eight year reign asserting German supremacy and restoring the Holy Roman Empire to its former power. This brought him to a constant state of war with the pope.

After first uniting the warring German Hohenstaufen and Welf (Guelph) factions, Frederick launched a series of invasions of northern Italy and Sicily. He was excommunicated by Pope Alexander III in 1160. Although triumphant in many battles, Frederick clearly could not achieve dominance over the papacy, and in 1177, after his defeat at Legnano, he asked for the pope's forgiveness and sued for peace.

He spent the remainder of his reign establishing German feudalism, allowing his nobles a degree of autonomy that won him much admiration and loyalty.

Saladin (1137–1193)

Salah al-Din Yusuf ibn Ayyub, founder of the Ayyubid Dynasty and liberator of Jerusalem, was as much revered and admired by his Christian adversaries as by his Muslim subjects. He was born in Takrit, Iraq, of Kurdish parentage. His father al-Ayyub and his uncle Shirkuh attained prominence in the service of the sultan of Damascus, Nur-ed-Din. Saladin was appointed Nur-ed-Din's security chief in 1156. With his uncle Shirkuh, he deposed the Fatimid vizier in 1169, and himself became Egypt's ruler, bringing him to conflict with his mentor, Nur-ed-Din.

Upon Nur-ed-Din's death, Saladin became supreme ruler, and in 1187 he defeated the Christian army at Hattin and swept up Jerusalem and many Frankish towns into his kingdom. His stalemated war with Richard the Lionheart, while preserving his gains, marked his decline. He died a sickly warrior in his fifties a few months after Richard's departure.

Saladin was much admired by his Christian enemies for his humanity. In his first foray into Egypt with his uncle, Saladin was captured at Alexandria by Amalric, king of Jerusalem. While recuperating in the Frankish camp, he made many friends among his captors. As he besieged the fortress of Kerak during a great wedding within, he spared the newlyweds' apartments while he bombarded the rest of the castle. His merciful treatment of his Jerusalem captives further burnished his chivalrous reputation. He and Richard mutually respected each other through the many battles they fought.

The reality is that he was as generous as he was cruel. He brutally slaughtered Cairo's Black Regiment and crucified Shi'ite and Fatimid rebels. He was not loath to create a spectacle of the execution of prisoners, laughing as his victims met their excruciating end. His mausoleum in Damascus contains two tombs, a common one built shortly after his death and a beautiful marble one, a gift of the German kaiser in honor of the chivalrous prince, as the West continues to view him.

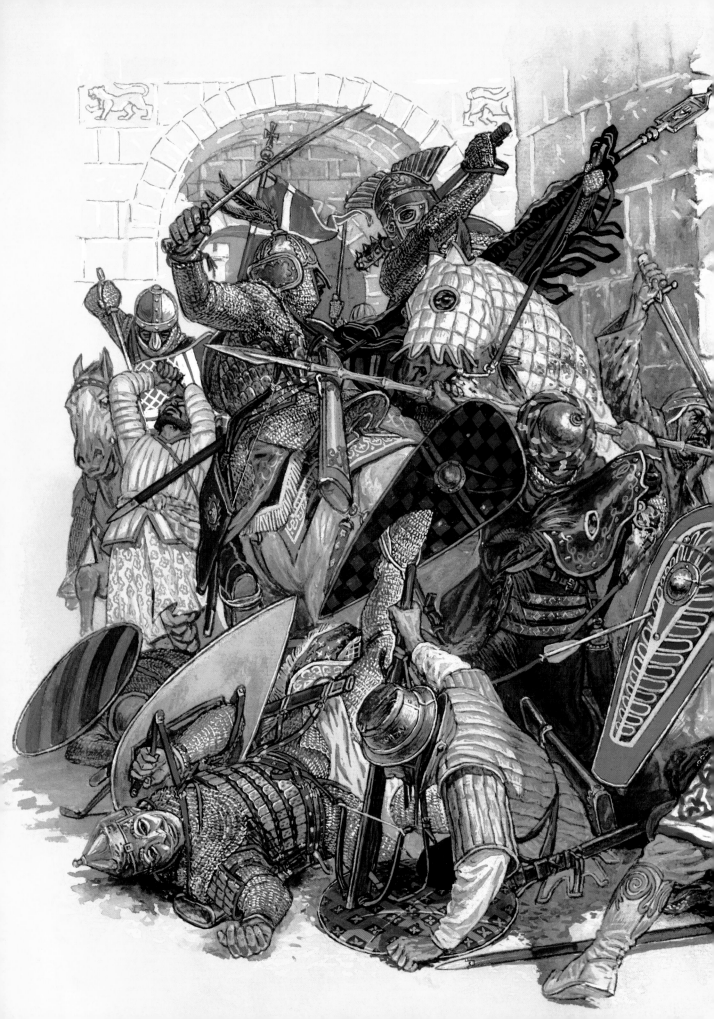

The Fourth Crusade:
The Sack of Constantinople
1202–1204

"The Fourth Crusade was an all-Christian war. Christian killed Christian, while not a single Saracen soldier was harmed."

With the approach of the thirteenth century the crusader states continued to maintain their tenuous hold on the Mediterranean coast. The Byzantine Empire had regained a portion of its territory lost to the Seljuk Turks at the battle of Manzikert in 1071. Venice had emerged as a major maritime power, and in 1199 a new pope Innocent III (1198–1216) was chosen.

Innocent III, with an overreaching ambition to consolidate all Christendom under his aegis, called for a new crusade. Venice was selected to transport the crusaders to the Holy Land. Venice was chosen because of its long relationship with the crusader states and the Byzantine Empire, its maritime prowess, and the fact that its rivals, Pisa and Genoa, were engaged in a major conflict with one another.

Venice had evolved in the eleventh and twelfth centuries into a prosperous trading center and maritime power. It was a republic ruled by a council, which was presided over by a doge. The doge, elected for life, at the time of the Fourth Crusade was eighty-year-old Enrico Dandolo (1192–1205). Dandolo, despite his advanced years, was an intelligent and vigorous leader.

A plan was set for the crusaders to gather in Venice from where they would set sail under the leadership of twenty-two-year-old Count Thibald of Champagne, brother of Henry Champagne, who had ruled the kingdom of Jerusalem from 1192 until his death in 1197. This crusade would be notable for the extreme youth of its leaders—few were over twenty-five.

Count Thibald's envoys negotiated with the wily Venetians to pay eighty-five thousand marks for the passage of 33,500 men to the Holy Land. The number of crusaders expected for transport was absurdly inflated, and consequently the amount of money promised excessive. Perhaps it was youthful

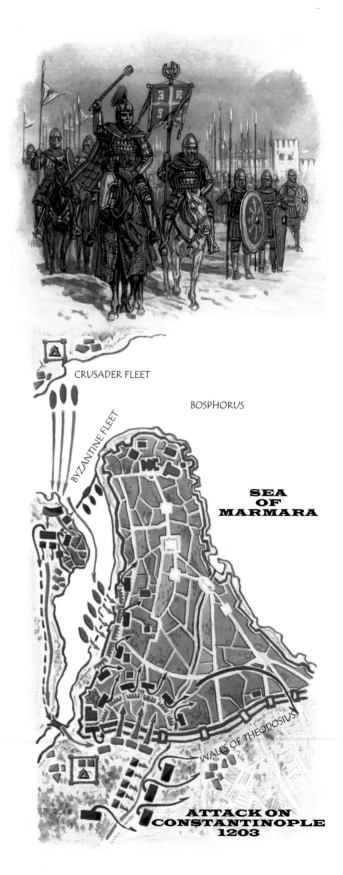

CRUSADER FLEET

BOSPHORUS

BYZANTINE FLEET

SEA OF MARMARA

WALLS OF THEODOSIUS

ATTACK ON CONSTANTINOPLE 1203

The usurper Alexis and Byzantine troops await the Frankish invasion. The first attack on Constantinople, July 5-7, 1203.

inexperience that led them to commit to such unreasonable terms.

A Change of Command

While Count Thibald's envoys were signing the agreements for ships, the count became ill and met an untimely death. Count Thibald's demise resulted in the election of Boniface of Montferrat to replace him. Boniface was the brother of Conrad of Montferrat who had been killed by Assassins in 1192 shortly after being named king of Jerusalem. Boniface was himself a young man.

The fleet that the Venetians had assembled was very large, some five hundred vessels, commensurate with the expectations of 33,500 men contracted for transport. The plan called for the crusade to depart in June 1202 at which time payments were to have been completed and all crusaders were to have arrived ready to sail for the Middle East. In fact, only token payment had been made by June, and only small numbers of the warriors of the cross had reached Venice.

French knights attack the Croation city Zadar.

Innocent III (1160–1216)

The first decade of the European thirteenth century was dominated by a vigorous pope whose efforts would consolidate ecclesiastical power and define the Roman Catholic religion for the next several centuries. Innocent was born Lotario Segni, scion of a powerful Italian family, well-bred and educated. He was not even a priest at the time of his election to Peter's throne as the youngest pope at age thirty-seven. It was a time when the spiritual authority of Rome was being challenged by popular heretical movements, its priests hated for greed and corruption, and its temporal authority besieged by various political factions seeking to use the pope as a pawn and religious authority as the cudgel.

The heretics were countered by the energetic preaching of two new orders, the Dominicans and Franciscans. When simple preaching failed, Innocent III authorized "crusades" that led to the massacre of the dissenters. The Albigensian crusade led by Simon de Montfort and northern French nobles against the Cathars in southern France was noted for its indiscriminate savagery.

Innocent was politically savvy and quite assertive. He was not afraid to use excommunication, and its implied eternal damnation, against monarchs who ignored his authority. King John of England was for a while an excommunicate until he came around to Innocent's points of view. Innocent aligned himself with the French crown, secured the thrones of Sicily and Germany for his young ward, Frederick II, and instigated the Fourth Crusade. Appalled at the sack of Constantinople in 1204, he excommunicated its participants but reaped the benefits of a Christendom united under the papacy. He restarted a quarrel begun by Frederick Barbarossa involving the German princes, whose right to elect the Holy Roman Emperor, Innocent claimed, was superseded by the pope's own right to veto an unacceptable candidate. Thus was born the Guelph (pro-papacy faction) versus Ghibelline (pro-emperor) wars that would fray Italy for almost two centuries.

He reduced the Church sacraments to seven, instituted the segregation of Jews who had to wear an identifying badge, centralized under papal control the creation of religious orders, the canonization of saints, and the annulment of marriages. He transformed the Inquisition from a local board of inquiry into heretical beliefs to a feared papal instrument of coercion. He presided over the Fourth Lateran Council of 1215 that defined many Catholic doctrines and practices, most of which are still observed today.

He died the most powerful man of his time, leaving the papacy a major political and military entity in European affairs for many years.

Most of the holy warrior volunteers who had arrived were French and numbered no more than eleven thousand, much fewer than promised. The money collected through the pope's taxes fell far short of the sum required by the Venetians. The entire endeavor was on the verge of collapse when Dandolo offered to render his city's maritime services at a lower rate if the crusaders would attack Zadar, a city on the Croatian coast recently captured from the Venetians by the Hungarian king.

The pope forbade this attack on another Catholic city held by a Catholic king under pain of excommunication. However, commerce trumped the fear of eternal damnation, and the Venetians and their French passengers sailed across the Adriatic and recaptured Zadar for the doge. They were immediately excommunicated and wintered and quarreled with each other in Zadar.

A Return to Byzantium

Along came a new cry for help from an exiled Byzantine prince. The Emperor Isaac II Angelus (1185–1195, 1203–1204) had been blinded and imprisoned by his brother, Alexius III (1195–1204). The young prince, also named Alexius, promised the crusaders a year's provisions and two hundred thousand silver marks to rescue his father. Dandolo coveted lucrative trading rights with Constantinople, and the crusaders needed financing. On June 5, 1203, after burning down Zadar, the Venetians and the French crusaders sailed for Byzantium, pledged to remove Alexius III and restore Isaac II to the throne, with insufficient thought to the enormous complexity of the task at hand.

The crusaders waited outside the city walls while the Venetians besieged the city by capturing its harbor fortifications. The usurper, Alexius, fled without a fight; the blind emperor and his son were reinstalled. Camped outside the city walls and anchored in the harbor, the crusaders and the Venetians waited to be paid. After a partial payment, it was soon clear that Prince Alexius could not deliver all the promised rewards. He asked the crusaders to stay for the winter while he collected taxes to make up the balance owed.

Picture to left: Warriors of the Fourth Crusade drive the Byzantine army out of Constantinople.

Having little choice, the invaders stayed and soon resentment between the foreigners and the local population turned to armed conflict, drunken brawls, and arson. No westerner was welcome within the city walls. The unpopular taxes intended as payment for the crusaders led to a palace coup, supported by most citizens. A commander of the palace guard named Alexius Murzuphlus (Alexius V, 1204) deposed the emperor and declared all previous agreements with the crusaders and Venetians invalid. Prince Alexius called on the crusaders to rescue him, but Murzuphlus forced him to drink poison.

The crusaders and their Venetian allies began a coordinated attack on the city. After several attempts, the Venetians scaled the ramparts on the masts of their ships while the crusaders successfully breached three gates. Murzuphlus took flight along with most of his army and the Greek nobility. The invaders were then allowed three days of rape and pillage throughout the city. No treasure, maiden, or priceless relic was spared. Those that resisted were slaughtered. The victorious

The Venetians Attack Constantinople

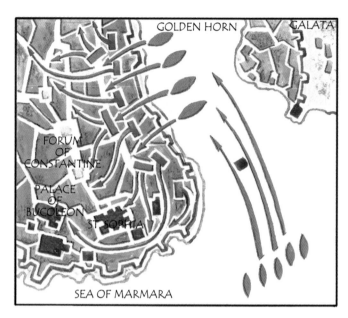

Above: Crusaders wade ashore outside Constantinople's walls.
Above right: The second attack on Constantinople, April 12, 1204.
Picture to right: A crusader knight breaks up a fight between French and Venetian troops.

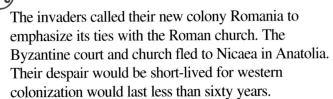

mob brought pack animals inside the Cathedral of St. Sophia to load up the precious plates, chalices, icons, and the rich vestments. A whore sat on the patriarch's throne and sang a bawdy soldier's song. Thus was Orthodox Christianity's holiest site defiled with lewdness, greed, and manure. Everyone had his proper portion of booty. The western prelates acquired an even greater share, uncovering caches of sacred relics, items of the greatest value in this era.

The New Kingdom

At the end of the rampage, the crusader and Venetian leaders sat together to choose a new emperor and patriarch. Baldwin IX, Count of Flanders and Hainault, Venice's candidate, became Emperor Baldwin I (1204–1205). The pope condemned the sack of Constantinople, but was nevertheless quite pleased that the Greeks were finally brought to heel. The empire was subdivided into enclaves—Venice colonized western Greece and Crete; Boniface became king of Thessalonica, vassal to the new Latin emperor; and the French took control of the eastern provinces including parts of Anatolia.

The invaders called their new colony Romania to emphasize its ties with the Roman church. The Byzantine court and church fled to Nicaea in Anatolia. Their despair would be short-lived for western colonization would last less than sixty years.

The Fourth Crusade witnessed the disintegration of the crusader ideals; chivalry and religious principles became secondary considerations. From its inception, the Fourth Crusade's focus became commercial rather than altruistic. It is estimated that the plunder from the sack of Constantinople was in excess of nine hundred thousand silver marks.

Though some crusaders reached Palestine, where their welcome was lukewarm at best, many more stayed in Greece or returned home. The Fourth Crusade was an all-Christian war. Christian killed Christian, while not a single Saracen soldier was harmed.

Instead of stemming the tide of Islamic warriors, the destruction of the Byzantine Empire assured the eventual desolation of the crusader states and secured the eventual dominance of the Ottoman Turks.

The Fifth Crusade:
Disaster on the Nile
1217–1221

"Pope Innocent III envisioned the recapture of the Holy Sepulcher as the crowning achievement of his life, and in 1213 began to send preachers to roil the masses once again."

The popular piety of the twelfth and thirteenth centuries maintained at its core the premise that the poor and meek, those not afflicted with affluence or prospects, would indeed inherit the earth. This constant sermonizing by the preachers of the period had led to the disastrous "People's Crusade" of 1096, and in 1212 gave rise to what became known as the Children's Crusade.

The Children's Crusade

It was during this time that a disorganized movement of children arose, whipped up by two lads, one a young shepherd named Stephen from Vendôme, and the other named Nicholas from Cologne. Their similar visions of Jesus had assured each that only the innocence of children would be deserving of victory over the Saracens. In 1212, children left their homes and followed these precocious preachers on the long trek to Jerusalem. At its peak thousands of children were engaged in this bizarre undertaking of the rescue of Jerusalem and the Holy Sepulcher from the Saracens through innocent faith instead of swords. Many joined the throng—the poor, the elderly, the occasional cleric, and children! Authorities were at a loss as to how to deal with this fervid mob, as any critic was deemed a heretic, a disbeliever, or just plain jealous.

The crowds of children took various routes, many actually finding passage on ships that were lost to pirates or to rocky shores, others walking the traditional roads to Constantinople, falling prey to kidnappers.

The Children's Crusade came to an end in a whimper. Those few children who were able to retrace their steps toward home faced an almost impossible journey. Where they had been celebrated on their way to the Holy Land, the returning children were now reviled and ridiculed. Many children ended up settling at whatever point where they could go no farther. Few children ever saw their families again; most of those who lived ended up enslaved.

The Fifth Crusade

The decade after the taking of Constantinople was one of peace in the Holy Land. The truce negotiated with al-Adil, Saladin's brother and successor, was honored by both sides, giving the adversaries a needed respite from the continuous warfare of the last forty years. In Palestine, after the deaths of various relatives of Guy of Lusignan, the crown of the nonexistent kingdom of Jerusalem based in Acre was placed on the head of John of Brienne, a Frenchman who had married the young queen, Maria of Montferrat. John was the personal choice of King Philip of France who had been asked to name a male ruler for Outremer.

The failure to recapture Jerusalem continued to haunt the powerful Pope Innocent III. However, the enthusiasm for crusading warfare had waned both in Europe and in Christian Outremer. The Christian port cities began to flourish as commercial centers, and the Frankish communities and their Muslim neighbors started to enjoy a tolerant coexistence once again. The few offers of military assistance from Western Europe were politely refused. The major conflicts were among the trading powers of Venice, Genoa, and Pisa.

Pope Innocent III envisioned the recapture of the Holy Sepulcher as the crowning achievement of his life, and in 1213 began to send preachers to roil the masses once again. He reinstated taxes to raise money for a new crusade. Momentum for a new expedition gathered under King Andrew of Hungary, but Innocent died in 1216 before seeing another Christian army depart. Volunteers from Hungary, Austria, Scandinavia, and the counties of Holland gathered at the Croatian port of Split. This time there were too few ships to carry the regiments and many returned home.

The fleet that reached Acre disgorged a smaller force than was needed to challenge the Muslims. King Andrew deemed that his crusader vows had been fulfilled and returned home, leaving command of the army to the king of Jerusalem, John of Brienne.

Picture to right: Khorezmian Turks overwhelm Jerusalem's garrison on August 23, 1244.

A larger force under Frederick II, the Holy Roman Emperor (1212–1250), was expected. King John temporized, not really desiring to destroy the lucrative coexistence with his Syrian neighbors. A minor attack on a Saracen outpost on Mt. Tabor that was unsuccessful served to occupy the visitors' time.

The Siege of Damietta

Commercial interests now became intermingled with renewed crusading zeal. The powerful Italian merchants had long desired control of the Egyptian port of Alexandria. They successfully convinced the Frankish commanders that the key to Jerusalem's recapture was the conquest of Egypt. Of course, a byproduct of such an invasion would certainly be the capture of Alexandria. So, to the astonishment of Sultan al-Adil and his son al-Kamil, Egypt's governor, King John sailed in May 1218 with the crusader army to besiege the Nile delta fortress city of Damietta with its seventy thousand inhabitants. It was a surprise to the Ayyubid rulers that the Christians would sacrifice the mutually enriching peace that had taken hold over the past decade, especially without any Muslim provocation to justify it. In fact, Sultan al-Adil died of shock at the news. His son al-Kamil became sultan while his other son al-Mu'azzam became the ruler of Syria.

Saracen forces scouting the enemy.

Cardinal Pelagius of Albano Takes Command

The badly organized siege lasted eighteen months in spite of reinforcements from France, Italy, England, and Spain. The Latin host would grow to more than forty thousand, but the city ringed with three walls withstood the encirclement. The papal legate, a Spanish cardinal named Pelagius, arrived in September 1218, insisting on taking command of the operation. Al-Kamil, still hoping to return to the peaceful and lucrative status quo, offered to return the entire kingdom of Jerusalem including the Holy City except for Transjordan. To keep this key land bridge between Egypt and Syria, he offered the Franks a yearly tribute.

Pelagius refused this offer to the consternation of all. Here, the Holy City was being handed over to Christian control with no further bloodshed, but Pelagius preferred to annihilate Islam altogether. As the siege continued in the dampness of the Nile delta, both besiegers and besieged were struck down with various tropical diseases. As much as twenty percent of the Christian army was lost to disease.

For months, the crusaders remained on the opposite bank from the fortress. A tall, fortified tower garrisoned with three thousand men had stood between the crusaders and the city. Although this tower was soon captured, the Egyptians blocked any further crossing with sunken ships. Even after defeating a Christian force outside Damietta in August, al-Kamil again repeated his offer of peace, additionally offering to rebuild Jerusalem's walls and returning the revered relic of the True Cross last seen at Hattin. Pelagius still refused.

The depleted Christian army finally crossed the Nile and camped under Damietta's walls. Damietta, itself reduced to a sepulcher of three thousand souls, finally capitulated in November 1219.

The Defeat at Mansourah

Twenty months after the victory, Pelagius was still waiting for the Emperor Frederick and his troops at Damietta. Some contingents of Italian and Teutonic knights did arrive, but not Frederick's mighty host. The exasperated Pelagius ordered a march up the Nile to Cairo. In July 1221, an army of six thousand crusaders marched south accompanied by a fleet of six

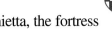

hundred boats. Forty miles from Damietta, the fortress of Mansourah stood in his way.

The Sultan al-Kamil once again offered favorable peace terms, which were again refused. The crusaders camped on a narrow spit of land marking the confluence of two branches of the Nile, opposite Mansourah.

With incessant rain, the river began to rise. While Saracen galleys blocked any retreat, the sultan added to the misery by ordering the breaching of dikes. The Christians watched as the river flooded their camp, and in great fear of drowning, petitioned for peace. Pelagius had already escaped on a galley headed back to Damietta. Al-Kamil allowed the survivors to withdraw and agreed to a truce of eight years provided the Christians left Damietta never to return. The sultan offered them the consolation of the relic of the True Cross to take back with them, but it could not be found. Pelagius, King John, and the rest of the Franks cleared out of Damietta that September. Al-Kamil entered the city in triumph.

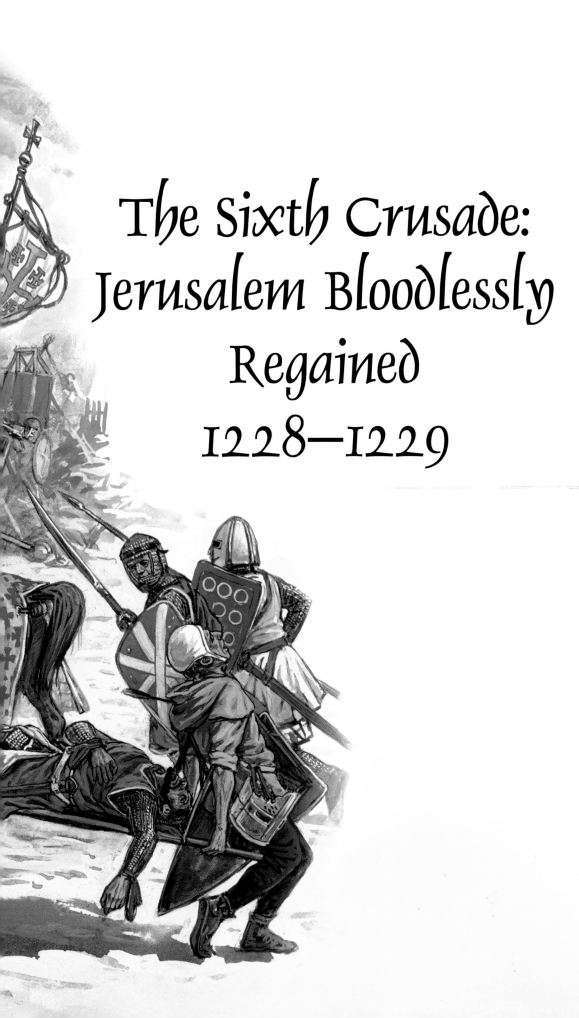

The Sixth Crusade: Jerusalem Bloodlessly Regained 1228–1229

"Frederick, the excommunicate, crowned himself the king of Jerusalem in the Church of the Holy Sepulcher. The barons of Outremer shunned him; the patriarch in Acre forbade any church services for him. Both sides of the Palestinian conflict had felt betrayed."

The Sixth Crusade was a curious episode. It was a sideshow to the greater conflict between the pope and the German Holy Roman Emperor. In addition, there was little warfare and bloodshed, a great deal of conniving diplomacy, and the Christians actually regained Jerusalem.

The Rivalry Between Church and State

Frederick II, grandson of Frederick I Barbarossa, was a man born three centuries too early. He was, in essence, the prototype Renaissance Machiavellian prince, a learned man who spoke six languages including Arabic, and a ruthless adversary to anyone in his way. He was called "Stupor Mundi," the Wonder of the World.

The rivalry between pope and emperor had been simmering for more than a century. Who controlled whom was the gist of the struggle. The Holy Roman Emperor was the most powerful man in the Western world. After a youth spent battling rivals and usurpers, Frederick in 1220 was crowned Holy Roman Emperor, ruler of the German regions and southern Italy. At his coronation he also took up the cross. Honorius III (1216–1227), Innocent's successor, urged him to sail with his powerful army to consolidate the foothold in Egypt, but the emperor had his own timetable and never left to fight in the Fifth Crusade. Pelagius, the papal legate, gave up waiting for him and proceeded up the Nile without him to suffer final defeat at Mansourah. Frederick continued to ignore the pope and set about consolidating his Italian possessions.

With ten years having passed since Frederick had made his commitment to the pope to take up the cross and recapture the Holy Land for Christendom, the acrimony between the Holy Roman Emperor and the papal prince had escalated year by year.

To further assuage the pope and confirm his intention of crusading, the widowed Frederick married the thirteen-year-old daughter of the king of Jerusalem, John Brienne. King John of Jerusalem was opposed to the nuptials, as he rightly feared the loss of his crown to Frederick. John Brienne had married Marie of Monteferrat, heiress to the kingdom. After her death in 1211 he, as guardian of his daughter Isabella, ruled as king of Jerusalem. John finally acquiesced to the marriage as a result of pressure from the pope as well as assurances from Frederick that he would not claim the throne of Jerusalem as Isabella's husband. The wedding took place in November 1225 and promptly thereafter Frederick declared himself king of Jerusalem, and yet he still refused to begin the crusade.

Finally, Frederick promised the exasperated Honorius that he would leave in August 1227. Honorius died early that year. Frederick's fleet did sail that August, but soon returned with a seriously ill emperor. Honorius' successor, Gregory IX (1227–1241), could stand no more procrastination and excommunicated Frederick in 1228.

As Frederick's health improved, he once more delayed his departure for the Holy Land to await the birth of his and Isabella's child, a son. Regrettably Isabella died in childbirth, complicating Frederick's claim to the throne of the kingdom of Jerusalem.

Never one to let unwanted details bar his way, such as the fact that the true king of Jerusalem was his son Conrad and Frederick could only be regent, Frederick finally set sail for the Holy Land in June 1228 to claim his kingdom.

Frederick's Crusade

For almost two years Frederick had been in secret negotiations with al-Kamil, sultan of Egypt, who was seeking Latin help against his ambitious brother, al-Mu'azzam, sultan of Syria. Al-Kamil had again offered the return of Jerusalem to the Christians in exchange for an alliance. This was in essence the same deal that Cardinal Pelagius rejected at Damietta.

When Frederick finally arrived in Acre with three thousand men, he was told that al-Kamil no longer needed his help. His brother, al-Mu'azzam, was now dead and the deal was off. At once pleading and threatening, Frederick was able to convince al-Kamil to abide by the original agreement after a prearranged Christian show of force and subsequent "negotiations." Frederick had cleverly disguised the relative weakness of his forces and bluffed his powerful adversary into signing away what his uncle, Saladin, had so gloriously achieved.

Without a single battle and without a single drop of blood spilled, Jerusalem, Bethlehem, and Nazareth were returned to the Frankish fold. A corridor linking the northern port cities with Jerusalem was agreed to, while the Dome of the Rock and the al-Aqsa mosque would stay in Muslim hands. These 1229 agreements would be binding for ten years.

Frederick, the excommunicate, crowned himself the king of Jerusalem in the Church of the Holy Sepulcher. The barons of Outremer shunned him; the patriarch in Acre forbade any church services for him. Both sides of the Palestinian conflict had felt betrayed. The Outremer warriors could not countenance a crusade that did not shed Saracen blood, while the Muslims reviled al-Kamil for giving away Jerusalem.

Frederick departed for home less than three months later upon hearing the news that the pope and his father-in-law, ex-King John, had invaded his Italian territories. He would never return to the kingdom he won without a fight. As he sailed away, crowds shouted insults and hurled rubbish at him.

Still, his was the craftiest, most cunning victory of all. *Stupor Mundi!*

Frederick II (1194–1250)

Grandson of Frederick Barbarossa and son of Constance of Sicily and Emperor Henry VI, Richard the Lionheart's jailer, Frederick was the most learned and most Machiavellian monarch of his century. He was crowned the king of Sicily at age three, entrusted to Pope Innocent III's guardianship by his mother. Throughout his life, Frederick considered himself Italian in spite of his German lineage. He was a highly educated man who spoke six languages.

Upon attaining his majority at fourteen, Frederick began consolidating what would become his empire. Innocent arranged his marriage to Constance of Aragon, with whose resources Frederick was able to acquire military power to subdue the various rebellions in Sicily. He faced the invading army of Otto, the king of Germany, who years earlier had murdered Frederick's uncle, Philip of Swabia in the struggle for the crown. Otto was excommunicated by the pope, shamed into retreat, and went home to be deposed by the council of German princes. They then handed the crown to young Frederick in 1210.

When his guardian Innocent died in 1216, Frederick's problems with the papacy started. Frederick continued the consolidation of his rule in Germany, appointing his son Henry the king of Germany in 1220 to the new Pope Honorius' chagrin. To salve the pope's anger, Frederick supported Rome in the persecution of heretics and promised to embark on a crusade. As a result, the pope recognized his election as Holy Roman Emperor and crowned him in Rome in 1222.

When Frederick, who was widowed in 1222, showed no signs of going to Palestine, the pope found him a new wife, Isabella of Brienne, the daughter of King John of Jerusalem. Frederick got her pregnant, imprisoned her, detained her father, and proclaimed himself king of Jerusalem. Still, he did not go on a crusade. Honorius died and Frederick once again promised the new pope, Gregory IX, a new crusade, but fell ill before he could set sail. He was excommunicated but won back Jerusalem while still in the state of excommunication.

During his absence, while in the Holy Land, the pope encouraged rebellion in Frederick's realm, supported by the northern Lombard League that sent an invasion force to Sicily. Frederick returned and forcefully put down these revolts, but spared the papacy any retribution. For this, the pope gratefully rescinded his excommunication.

The rest of his life was spent in intermittent wars with the pope who saw in Frederick's ascendant power in Italy a grave threat to papal supremacy. Even his son, Henry, joined in a revolt by German barons in 1234, which Frederick quickly quelled, sending his son to a lifetime of captivity in Sicily.

After another excommunication by Gregory, Frederick invaded the papal states. A stalemate ensued between the rivals, each of whom captured hostages. When Gregory died in 1241, negotiations with his successor Innocent IV appeared to bear fruit but collapsed. In 1247, a papal conclave affirmed the anathema against Frederick. Some branded him the antichrist, and any oath of obedience and loyalty to him was invalidated.

The last years of his life were spent in reversing setbacks he had suffered in northern Italy. He died of dysentery on December 12, 1250, in Apulia and was buried in Palermo, Sicily. Many did not believe the veracity of his death, and like some latter day rock stars, he was reported seen alive in this place and that for many years after.

A man of intimidating knowledge, an enthusiastic sponsor of the arts and sciences, and a stern ruler and lawgiver, Frederick, "Stupor Mundi," was much admired by those who saw in him a firm bulwark against the ambitious papacy. Many hoped for a long dynasty that would bring a renaissance, but Frederick's line ended eighteen years later. Charles of Anjou, the brother of Louis IX, took Sicily in 1266, defeating Frederick's bastard son, Manfred, and in 1268, captured the last heir, Conradin, and executed him.

St. Louis and The Seventh Crusade: Jerusalem Lost Forever
1248–1254

"King Louis of France, deathly ill with malaria, vowed to rescue Jerusalem if his life was spared. Jerusalem had faded as Christianity's emerald city, and crusading was seen in many circles as a waste of time and treasure, its preaching the pope's bad breath."

During the decade of peace that followed Frederick's crusade, the Outremer ports of Acre and Tyre thrived as commercial centers for the Mediterranean trade. The growing prosperity shared with their Syrian trading partners ensured that peace would be of mutual interest.

Prelude: Thibald's Adventure

This triumph of secular materialism was not appreciated in Europe where the pope continued to stoke crusading zeal, calling for the annihilation of Islam, treaty or no treaty. Frederick successfully lobbied his adversary to wait at least until the ten-year treaty expired before sending new contingents to the East.

Christianity was riven with family conflict throughout its realms. Frederick and Pope Gregory IX (1227-1241) had an on-again, off-again war in Italy. The Latin empire of Constantinople was under great pressure from the shadow Greek court in exile at Nicaea and the rebellious Balkan Slavs in the north. And in Jerusalem the Outremer barons refused to recognize Frederick's representatives.

Al-Kamil, the Ayyubid sultan of Egypt who had negotiated the ten-year treaty with Frederick II, died in 1238, the year before the treaty expired, setting off a struggle for succession between Cairo and Damascus. With the death of al-Kamil, his kingdom was divided between his two sons: al-Salih in Damascus and al-Adil ruling in Cairo. The jealous, ambitious brothers would be locked in determined effort to wrest each other's territory to become sole ruler of their father's former kingdom. The Saracens were not yet ready to reclaim Jerusalem, but the pope did not wait to send new French and English regiments under Thibald of Champagne, king of Navarre, and Richard of Cornwall to restart hostilities. They reached Acre in September 1239, met by the rebellious commune of barons who had rejected Frederick's rule.

The newly arrived French and English army, combining with local warriors with a strength of four thousand men, marched south to claim the unused ruins of Ascalon. In the course of the expedition, one of Thibald's lieutenants, Peter of Dreux, and two hundred of his men left the main column and captured a large herd of animals being driven to Damascus. Not to be outdone, Henry of Bar, ignoring the counsel of local nobles, left camp at midnight to ambush an Egyptian detachment reported to be near Gaza. His force of five hundred was annihilated in a skirmish on the sand dunes. A small group of horsemen was all that returned to the main body, which returned dispirited to Acre.

The demoralized Christian force did not even stir when Jerusalem was attacked, albeit unsuccessfully. Then a convoluted sequence of events delivered a measure of success to Thibald's expedition. Approached by al-Salih of Damascus who was at war with his brother, the new ruler in Cairo, Thibald agreed to an alliance in return for Beaufort Castle, Sidon, Tiberias, Safad, Galilee, Bethlehem, large areas of southern Palestine, and the continuation of Christian control of Jerusalem. The only condition was victory over the Egyptians.

The alliance proved so unpopular that when the forces rendezvoused at Jaffa, the Damascene army refused to march south and returned home. Thibald then turned to Cairo and offered a nonaggression treaty in exchange for southern Palestine. With Cairo's agreement in principle, Thibald then left for home.

A small force under Richard, earl of Cornwall, brother of Henry III of England, had already sailed to Acre, arriving in October 1240 after Thibald's departure. Richard confirmed Thibald's treaty with Egypt adding all of Galilee to the package. Outremer was now restored to its greatest boundaries since Hattin. This second zenith would last a mere three years.

The Second Fall of Jerusalem

The Ayyubid empire was disintegrating in disunity, Cairo warring against Damascus just as new invaders appeared from the east. Genghis Khan's Mongol armies were again advancing westward, driving the Khorezmian Turks in the thousands from their territories south of the Aral Sea into Syria.

It was unfortunate that the Franks were themselves nearing civil war. Factions of various loyalties fought each other in the Christian cities. Templars and Hospitallers crossed swords in the streets of Acre. Acre fought Tyre. Still, the sultans of Cairo and Damascus each sought an alliance with the Franks to vanquish the other. The Christians decided to support Damascus. Cairo turned to the Khorezmian Turks.

Egypt loosed ten thousand Turkish horsemen on Damascus in June 1244. Damascus was still the tough fortress it was during the Second Crusade, and the frustrated Turks turned southwest and attacked

Crusaders charge the Egyptian sultan's Ghulams soon after landing at Damietta.

Jerusalem on August 23, 1244, easily overwhelming its puny defenses. The Christians' sacred places were pillaged and burned. The slaughter spared but three hundred of six thousand Christians within. With Jerusalem devastated, the Turks joined the Egyptian army at Gaza. At the village of La Forbie, a few miles northeast, their combined forces annihilated a Christian–Damascene army. It was the largest loss of crusader life since Hattin. Only a few hundred Frankish warriors were left in all of Outremer.

Louis IX of France

King Louis of France, deathly ill with malaria, vowed to rescue Jerusalem if his life was spared. His was the only fevered response to the loss of the Holy City among the European rulers. Jerusalem had faded as Christianity's emerald city, and crusading was seen in many circles as a waste of time and treasure, its preaching the pope's bad breath. Pilgrims returning from Palestine were more impressed by the civilized

Louis IX's troops capture the Egyptian camp outside Mansourah.

Muslims than many of the Christian who infested Tyre and Acre.

Nevertheless, Louis recovered and spent the next three years preparing his crusade. The Church financed two-thirds of the cost; the rest came from taxes and the treasure taken from Jews and heretics. Louis was a great planner, and logistics for the expedition were well thought through. The vast fleet set sail in August 1248, carrying around twenty thousand mostly French troops. Upon arrival in Cyprus they saw the abundant supplies already prepositioned by Louis' strategic planning. Louis' plan imitated that of the Fifth Crusade—to recapture Jerusalem from the south by gaining Egypt.

Damietta and Mansourah Once Again

After wintering in Cyprus, Louis arrived with an advance detachment off Damietta in June 1249. The impatient Louis landed, with the main body of his fleet still miles behind. The sultan's forces retreated after some token resistance and abandoned the city to the French. Louis gathered his army and stayed in Damietta for five months to avoid the Nile floods that doomed Pelagius less than three decades earlier and to wait for his brother Alphonse of Poitiers to arrive with more troops.

Louis' war council led by another brother, Robert of Artois, opted to subjugate the Nile Valley, thus controlling Egypt and forcing the Muslims to withdraw from Jerusalem. Taking the same route that John Brienne and Cardinal Pelagius of Albano used in 1221, the army, joined by Templars and Hospitallers, marched on the left bank of the Nile followed by supply boats. They were harassed every step of the way by shadowing Egyptian warriors. Learning from Richard the Lionheart, Louis strictly forbade the breaking of ranks, although the Templars disregarded the royal edict, slaying some Arab horsemen who came too close. As in 1221, they were stopped at the fortified town of Mansourah on the opposite bank outside whose walls encamped a large Egyptian force. There was no choice but to assail this strategic barrier.

While the Christians began to build a causeway across the river, the Egyptians launched barrels of Greek fire at their handiwork. As soon as the French extended their bridge, the Egyptians dug away the earth on their side, leaving their enemy no closer. The adversaries settled down to daily artillery duels with catapults and slings when a Bedouin offered to show the Christians a ford downriver where they could cross and outflank their enemy. This was a godsend because the Egyptians had reduced river traffic carrying supplies from Damietta, and the Muslim cavalry was nipping at the crusaders' rear.

On February 7, 1251, the Christians made an orderly though difficult crossing at the ford, Louis expressly commanding all units to keep in close contact and to advance only on his orders. The ford was a little deeper than desired, the opposite bank steep and slippery with mud, and some men-at-arms and their mounts drowned. As the vanguard made it safely across, a group of three hundred Muslim horsemen came on the scene. Robert of Artois, ignoring his brother's orders, charged with his detachment. The Templars, not to be outdone, attacked as well, giving chase all the way to the Egyptian camp. The Christian cavalry did surprise the Egyptians who were cut down as they tried to don their armor and mount their horses.

Sensing an easy victory, Count Robert ordered an immediate attack on the town against the better judgment of the Templar Master and of the Earl of Salisbury. Their manhood questioned, they sallied forth behind Robert while he met destruction in the narrow streets of the town. When Louis heard about his brother's senseless death, he advanced upon the camp only to face a regrouped force of Egyptians. He had wisely ordered a bridge to be quickly made while the army was fording the river. In the evening, infantry reinforcements poured over the newly completed span, and the Muslims fled leaving Louis to claim a Pyrrhic victory.

The Egyptian army soon regrouped and harassed Louis' positions. He was trapped at Mansourah. For four months, his army camped on both banks of the Nile, cut off from their supplies at Damietta and surrounded by Egyptian soldiers or Egyptian waters. Disease festered among the Europeans, exacerbated by hunger and fierce attacks by their tormentors. The decision was made to march back to Damietta.

The ragged columns made it only as far as Farskur, far short of Damietta. Louis, deathly ill, was captured among the rearguard. After lengthy negotiations, Damietta was returned to Muslim control and a large ransom of 800,000 gold bezants was to be paid for the release of Louis and his surviving knights. Louis did not have enough in his treasury to pay even half of the required sum. The

Templars lent the king enough for fifty percent, with the Egyptians agreeing to wait for the rest.

Louis returned to Acre in May 1250 and stayed in the Holy Land for another four years. There he was accepted as the de facto king in the absence of Frederick II's son, Conrad IV. Louis supervised the improvement of the Christian-fortified cities and carried out diplomatic offensives that won a temporary alliance with his former Egyptian captors who even forgave the remaining half of his ransom.

He also sent envoys to the Mongol emperor Mongka at Karakorum. Now the world's superpower ruling an empire that began in China and expanded west to Russia, Genghis Khan's descendants were viewed by the Franks as potential allies in their struggle for survival. It was widely believed that among the Mongol hordes were Christians, including some generals. Louis' envoys were welcomed at the Khan's court, but their goodwill gifts were taken as tribute and the envoys were sent back to tell the French

king that henceforth his gift giving would be an annual event. He was now their vassal.

Many Mongols were indeed Nestorian Christians, belonging to a sect that followed the teachings of a heretical fifth century patriarch of Constantinople, Nestorius, who believed that Jesus was actually two persons, one human and one divine. The great Khan's mother was Christian and so were several of his wives. But to him, Christianity was merely one of many religions whose leaders swore allegiance to him.

When the Mongol army began to move westward once more in 1256 under the emperor's brother Hulegu, the Christians fared better than the other wretched souls in their way. But an enemy more cunning than they had ever faced before awaited the advancing Mongols: the Mamluks.

The retreat from Mansourah.

Mamluks, Mongols, and the Eighth Crusade

1270

"It was remarkable how quickly disease took hold in the Christian camp. Typhus, malaria, and dysentery spared neither peasant nor noble. Louis watched his son, the Count of Nevers, die while he himself began to suffer fevers. King Louis IX died whispering Jerusalem, Jerusalem..."

The Egyptian army that held Louis captive after Mansourah was no longer led by Arabs. While the crusaders were marching on Mansourah, the powerful, old sultan Ayub died in Cairo, a fact kept secret from the garrison. The new sultan, Turranshah, was assassinated by leaders of his bodyguard, the Mamluks. The Mamluks would rule Egypt as an independent dynasty until 1517 and as Ottoman vassals until Napoleon arrived in 1798.

The End of the Ayyubid Dynasty

The Arab word *mamluk* denoted a slave chosen as a child to be raised as a professional warrior. In the ninth century, the Egyptian Fatimids had started the practice of rounding up young boys from the nomad peoples of Central Asia to train as elite cavalry dedicated to the protection of the sultan. By the twelfth century, the Mamluks were mostly Turkish, although some may have been former Christian captives. These skilled mounted warriors formed the core of most Muslim armies that faced the Franks. Although converts to Islam, Mamluks never assimilated into local society. They lived in their barracks, few spoke Arabic, and most married enslaved Turkish women or daughters of Mamluks.

In 1250, amid the confusion of the sultan's death and a crusader invasion, the Mamluks overthrew their masters. They set up a military regime under their first sultan, Aybak. Among the circle of leaders was an ambitious and charismatic warrior rumored to have been knighted several years earlier by Frederick II, Baybars Bundukdari. He ascended to the sultanate in 1260 as the third sultan after murdering the second, Qutuz. Baybars would help drive the Mongols out of the Holy Land, and as sultan he would be the final undoing of the Outremer kingdom.

Battle of Ayn Jalut

The great Mongol General Hulegu's campaign in 1258 had gone quite successfully. Relentless as modern-day blitzkrieg, his combined arms formations destroyed the Persian base of the Assassins at Alamut and defeated the caliph of Baghdad's army. His Mongols massacred eighty thousand Muslims in the sack of the fabled city, but spared all its Christians. The powerful Abbasid caliph who was the nominal head of the Islamic world was executed along with most of his family. Conquering every city in its westward path, Hulegu's army finally crossed the Euphrates, reaching the gates of Aleppo in 1259. Hethoum, King of Armenia, and Bohemond, Prince of Antioch, met Hulegu to pay him homage and to cement an alliance against the Muslims. These two local lords accompanied Hulegu's Christian General Kitbogha in the bloody taking of Damascus.

The sudden death of the Great Khan at Karakorum ended any further advance by the Mongol army. By Genghis Khan's edict, all the Mongol leaders, including Hulegu, were required to return to the capital to choose a new Khan. Kitbogha was left with a substantial but reduced force to hold Damascus and the surrounding Mongol territories, which extended as far as Gaza.

The idea of a Mongol alliance was no longer a popular idea in the Christian cities. The ruthless killing of defeated civilians served to further demonize the

Louis IX's French knights attack the city of Tunis.

Conqueror, Baybars the Panther.

Asian hordes. And so, Qutuz, the second Mamluk sultan, was granted safe passage for his army through Christian territory on its way to confront the invaders in Syria. The Mongols had given Qutuz an opportunity to sign on as a full-fledged tribute-paying vassal, but the Mamluk sultan beheaded the unfortunate Mongol emissaries sent to Cairo and marched his army north, taking Gaza before obtaining the Christians' promise to be mere spectators in the coming battle.

On September 3, 1260, at Ayn Jalut (Pools of Goliath), north of Jerusalem, the Mamluk and Mongol armies met in battle. Kitbogha's force of ten thousand was not totally Mongol. Most were Turkish, Armenian, and Georgian levies. He did not have sufficient cavalry to do the thorough reconnaissance that was standard for Mongol campaigns and was slightly outnumbered by Qutuz' twelve thousand.

Baybars commanded the Mamluk vanguard that encountered the Mongols at dawn. He immediately feigned a retreat, fleeing from the Mongol arrow storm. Kitbogha gave immediate chase only to find himself surrounded in a valley by the rest of Qutuz' forces occupying the high ground. These were typical Mongol tactics now used against the Mongols. Kitbogha's soldiers fought ferociously, repeatedly counterattacking and succeeding in breaking the Mamluk left. An all-out charge led by Qutuz routed the Mongols, many of whom fled on foot up the surrounding hills, only to be cut down by dismounted ghulams. Kitbogha was captured and immediately beheaded.

Ayn Jalut was the first defeat suffered by the Mongols in a major battle after more than three decades of conquest. The Mamluks quickly retook Damascus and

Baybars the Panther

After the Mamluk victory at Ayn Jalut in 1260, Sultan Qutuz rebuffed Baybar's request to become a regional governor. When they returned to Egypt, Baybars once again approached Qutuz with a new request: to marry a beautiful captive woman. Qutuz bestowed his blessing and as Baybars kissed his hand in gratitude, his assassins slit the throat of Qutuz.

Born in Kipchak in the Volga valley of Mongol Russia in 1223, Baybars was kidnapped as a boy and sold in Damascus, but was returned because one of his blue eyes was blurred by a cataract. He acquired the surname Bundukdari ("belonging to the crossbowman") from an early owner. He was eventually purchased by the Ayyubid sultan and trained as a Mamluk. He rose in rank in the sultan's bodyguard. He was described as tall and swarthy with a strong voice and a violent temper. Above all, he was an energetic leader.

He directed a systematic expansion of the Mamluk empire, using both military and diplomatic means. It helped that the Mongol empire fragmented into individual khanates early in his reign. As he drove the Persian ilkhanate Mongols back across the Euphrates, his ambassadors cemented an alliance with the Golden Horde Mongols as leverage against their rival cousins in Baghdad. He unleashed an unrelenting and ruthless campaign to capture Christian towns while negotiating with the restored Byzantine Emperor Michael Paleologus in Constantinople to isolate the remaining Latin communities of Outremer.

Baybars' campaigns against the Franks were especially savage. From the Mongols he learned the value of a bloody and brutal reputation in weakening a foe's resolve. He would lead raids into Christian areas beheading every Frank he found. Caesarea, Haifa, and Arsuf were recaptured in 1265. The great Templar fortress at Safad fell the next year. Christian Cilicia was overrun as well. Jaffa, Beaufort, and the great city of Antioch were taken in 1268. The Hospitaller castle of Krac des Chevaliers and the bastion at Montfort were his by 1271. The defenders were either enslaved or beheaded.

Not just a military ruler, Baybars promoted the economic well-being of his kingdom by negotiating commercial treaties with Charles of Anjou, the king of Sicily and brother of Louis IX, Jaime of Aragon, and Alfonso of Seville. He rebuilt fortifications, shipyards, and mosques. Some of his public works projects still stand in Cairo. He established a postal system very similar to the American Pony Express. To ensure his realm's security, he built roads and bridges to link his various garrisons.

He died when his plot to poison an upstart rival, Malik Kaher, backfired. His intended victim switched glasses and Baybars took thirteen days to die a slow, excruciating death.

Aleppo and though the Mongols would remain in Turkish Anatolia for a few more decades, they never again would challenge Mamluk domination of the Holy Land.

The Byzantine Recapture of Constantinople

The fragmentation of Christian Outremer was mirrored in the decline of the Western European regime in Constantinople. After the heady victory in 1204, the old empire was divided into rival cantons. The Venetians and various French factions controlled defined territories.

In 1261, the Byzantine Emperor Michael VIII (1261–1282), operating from the exile capital of Nicaea, recaptured Constantinople, ending the brief Roman rule of its eastern Christian rival.

Louis IX and the Eighth Crusade

Louis returned to his French kingdom in 1254, haunted by his failure to recapture God's territories. For years he donated thousands of livres for the defense of Outremer. While the Mongols were sacking Baghdad and the cities of northern Syria, he began planning a return. But the pope was too busy cleansing Italy of Frederick II's progeny and influence, while Venice and Genoa waged a naval war for commercial supremacy. More than a decade would pass before the pope finally controlled Frederick's old kingdoms with the help of Louis' brother, Charles of Anjou, who was crowned King of Sicily. With all of Frederick's heirs dead, the pope began to actively support Louis' crusade in 1267.

In 1270, Louis IX set sail with ten thousand men. With him were three of his sons, his son-in-law, King Thibald of Navarre, and the sons of nobles who had suffered defeat with him in Egypt twenty years earlier. His brother, Charles of Anjou, planned to follow Louis. They had decided to capture Tunis, then proceed to Acre, which held on in the face of Baybars' incessant victories.

The choice of Tunis is a puzzle. Louis might have been led to believe that the emir of Tunis was ready to convert to Christianity with a show of force. Perhaps he decided to help his brother Charles in his feud with the emir over trade and the emir's support of the Hohenstaufen exiles from Sicily sheltering in Tunis. The crusaders landed on July 18 and set up camp on the site of ancient Carthage. A few Arab raids were turned back by Louis, but neither side gained any advantage.

It was remarkable how quickly disease took hold in the Christian camp. Typhus, malaria, and dysentery spared neither peasant nor noble. Louis watched his son, the Count of Nevers, die while he himself began to suffer fevers. King Louis IX died whispering "Jerusalem, Jerusalem…" in the humid royal tent outside Tunis on August 25, scarcely six weeks after landing.

His brother, Charles of Anjou, King of Sicily, reached Tunis as Louis lay dying. He shortly thereafter negotiated a treaty with the emir of Tunis and withdrew the sick remnants of Louis' army. The Eighth Crusade was over, its soldiers never reaching the Holy Land.

As Charles sailed homeward, Prince Edward, the future Edward I "Longshanks" of England and "Hammer of the Scots," arrived in Tunis with one thousand men. He proceeded to Acre to be joined by his brother, Edmund of Lancaster. Another pure warrior in the tradition of his Plantagenet predecessor, Richard the Lionheart, Edward took over the flagging resistance to Baybars, the Mamluk sultan. He convinced the Mongol ruler in Anatolia to attack Baybars in concert with his own raids.

Edward was not successful in these armed incursions into Mamluk territory, although Baybars must have felt threatened by this descendant of the Lionheart. He took out a contract on Edward's life with the Assassins who still operated in Syria only by Baybars' forbearance. (He would wipe them out in a few years.) Edward survived the assassination attempt in June 1272, but took ill for several months. Edward finally left in September to become England's king.

When Baybars died in 1277, he had reduced Outremer to the solitary bastion of Acre. Jerusalem was firmly back in Muslim control, but now existed as an unimportant garrison town in the hinterlands of the Mamluk empire, neglected by the sultan in Cairo. Tripoli, Jaffa, Antioch, the towns of Galilee, all had been emptied of their Christian citizens. Many sought refuge in Acre or Latakia in occupied Antioch, some fled to Cyprus or to the Byzantine regions. Few reached Western Europe. Many of these Outremer "Franks" were really more Middle Eastern than European. They would be strangers in the colder climes and cities of their ancestors.

Italian Commercial Rivalry and the Crusades

After the victories of the First Crusade, the competing interests of the Italian maritime powers, Genoa, Pisa, and Venice, came to control the politics and military decisions of the barons of Outremer. Trade and profit often overrode religious edict and made allies of those who would otherwise slit each other's throats. Passing alliances with Muslim powers would be struck if the profit margins required it.

In the early twelfth century, Italian ships were already plying a lucrative trade between their city-states and the Byzantine empire. Genoa enjoyed a head start. Her ships supported the First Crusade, her sailors captured Jaffa while the crusaders encircled Jerusalem and joined the siege and the sacking of the city.

The Genoese established an alliance with the crusaders, staking claim to a full third of the booty and a quarter of each town captured. The Pisans, allied with Byzantium, challenged the Genoese and steadily gained a good portion of the business. Italian trading outposts could be found as far as the Black Sea and the banks of the Danube.

The Italians provided seaborne passage to pilgrim and crusader while transporting timber and metal to Christian and Muslim ports. The Genoese maintained a monopoly on the slave trade. Ships returning westward carried spices, carpets, silk, and other goods delivered by Muslim caravans to the customs houses of the Middle Eastern port cities.

The competition for exclusive trading rights with the various cities from the Aegean to Alexandria in the southeastern corner of the Mediterranean turned to armed conflict on the high seas. In 1123, a large Venetian force of 120 ships drove off an Egyptian fleet and assisted in the retaking of Tyre. From then on, these three Italian republics would vie for commercial supremacy, enlisting allies wherever they could be found.

In the Third Crusade, the English supported the Pisans, while the French helped the Genoese. In the Fourth Crusade, Venice's crafty manipulation of the youthful crusader leadership advanced its own agenda and enriched the city beyond all expectations. Zadar was retaken from the Hungarians, and much of Constantinople's plundered treasures were piled up in Venetian palaces and churches. And they cornered the Byzantine trade for the next sixty years.

A great portion of Jerusalem's annual revenues were transferred to the Italian trading powers. This impoverishment and the divisive intrusion into the quarrels within the Christian kingdom eventually contributed to its fall.

The Fifth Crusade was diverted to Egypt because of the Italian interest in controlling the great port city of Alexandria. Each of the Christian cities had separate zones where Genoese, Pisans, and Venetians lived and worked. Brawls often turned into full battles. The Templars and the Teutonic Knights supported the Venetians, while the Hospitallers sided with the Genoese.

The maritime powers viewed any new crusade with both dread and anticipation. Armed conflict always brought with it the real possibility that carefully crafted trade agreements would be abrogated and the flow of goods interrupted. On the other hand, war was an opportunity to gain an advantage over Italian rivals by excluding them from booty or, even better, disrupting their trade routes. In the thirteenth century calls for crusade had therefore become unpopular because the peaceful flow of wealth from the East to the Italian trading powers would certainly be upset.

And so it was that while crusaders fought the Saracens, Italian sailors fought each other and negotiated with the enemy for commercial advantage. Open warfare between Venetians and Genoese allied with Pisans erupted in the streets of Acre in the War of St. Sabas in 1256. The Templars and Hospitallers predictably entered the fray. It took two years for the Venetians and their allies to drive the Genoese out of Acre. Later, as the Christian cities and towns fell to Baybars and his heirs, the Italian merchants continued to discuss trading arrangements with the Mamluks.

Pisa's share of the Mediterranean trade steadily declined through the 1200s. Its sun set when the Genoese defeated their fleet in 1284 in the Battle of Meloria off the Italian Tyrrhenian coast. Genoa and Venice would continue to compete well into the next century. Venice finally ratified its commercial domination over Genoa in the Peace of Turin signed in 1381. The Most Serene Republic became the major maritime power in the western Mediterranean for the next several centuries.

> *"When Baybars died in 1277, his successor, Qalawun, continued the dismantling of the Frankish kingdom. Marqab, the Hospitaller's last great fortress, was captured in 1285, Antioch's holdout port of Latakia was taken in 1287, and two years later, Tripoli. By 1290, only Acre remained."*

The rump kingdom of Jerusalem existed only as a thought in the still booming city of Acre. It still had a king, Hugh, who was crowned in 1269, only to give up the whole idea and flee to Cyprus in 1276. His rival, Maria of Antioch, sold the kingdom, or the paper rights to the concept, to Charles of Anjou, King of Sicily, who found no time to tend to it. There was no single unifying leader to direct the resistance to the Mamluks. The end was only a matter of time. In 1286 Hugh's son, Henry of Lusignan, then ruler of Cyprus, was crowned as the last king of Jerusalem.

Afterword

When Baybars died in 1277, his successor, Qalawun, continued the dismantling of the Frankish kingdom. Marqab, the Hospitaller's last great fortress, was captured in 1285, Antioch's holdout port of Latakia was taken in 1287, and two years later, Tripoli. By 1290, only Acre remained.

One last attempt at rescue was organized by Pope Nicholas IV. As much as he preached to congregations and begged the many monarchs of Europe, he could muster no more than a small English force and some commoners from Northern Italy under the nominal command of the displaced bishop of Tripoli. Ferried by twenty Venetian and five Aragonese galleys, this pitiful band reached Acre in August 1290 in the midst of a truce with Sultan Qalawun.

The newly arrived mob of Tuscans, Lombards, and Englishmen fought with Muslim merchants who continued to trade in the city in spite of the war. The brawls escalated into a full-scale massacre of Muslims in Acre. With this provocation, the sultan announced the end of the truce, but died before he could mount a final assault on this last Christian city. His son, al-Ashraf Khalil, carried out the planned siege, which began on April 5, 1291.

The city had improved its defenses since Baybars' failed attempt at its capture in 1267. For a month, Khalil rained arrows, Greek fire, and stones into the city from as many as sixty siege machines. King Henry arrived with reinforcements, but it was too late. Acre's citizens crowded the harbor side and begged the sailors on his ships to evacuate them.

Though many made it to safety in Cyprus, many more met their cruel fate in the final assault less than two weeks later. The massacre of Christians was unrestrained. Women and their babies were slain; soldiers who surrendered were beheaded. The Templars made one last stand in their coastal fortress. The Mamluks mined the towers which finally toppled into the sea. This was the Christian kingdom's dying gasp.

Epilogue

By the end of 1291, the cleansing of mainland Outremer was complete. Acre was totally demolished to prevent its future use; the entire Mediterranean coastline was denuded of crops and buildings. Excepting the unfortunate who were now slaves, no Frank called the Holy Land home. The nearest Christian center was Cyprus.

In 1297, Pope Boniface VIII declared Louis IX of France a saint despite his two failed attempts at rescuing Jerusalem. Perhaps it was a good decision at the time, but the pious and gentle Louis' hateful persecution of the Jews and his intention to convert or kill the Muslims no longer stand as exemplary virtues for Christian emulation.

Two new waves of conquerors would arise from the East and spend their allotted time on history's stage. The Ottoman Turks would sweep through Anatolia on their way to the gates of Vienna two centuries later. In time, even the Mamluks would become their vassals. Tamerlane would be a reincarnated Genghis Khan for his generation, but would leave no legacy after his death.

The crusading ideal would continue to affect European religious culture for two centuries after the last crusader departed the holy lands. The Teutonic Knights efficiently colonized and baptized the Baltic region, but would suffer utter defeat at Grunwald in

1410 when they confused conversion with conquest. The Christian Reconquista in the Iberian lands would be completed by Ferdinand and Isabella at the end of the fifteenth century. The remnants of the Hospitallers would be a bulwark against the Ottoman Empire well into the sixteenth century.

The bloodstained savagery unleashed by Christian fanaticism during the era of the Crusades was unequaled until the modern times. This brutality in the service of religion was copied and sharpened by the crusaders' Muslim enemies. Most of Christianity has since returned to the more tolerant and pacifist attitudes originally espoused by its founder. It is the tragedy and the great peril of our time that the example of cruel intolerance taught by the crusaders has not been abandoned by their original victims. In spite of our comfortable denials, civilizations and religions still war with each other, the killing more efficient than ever. And so, we continue to pay for the sins of the Crusades.

"Muslim armor paralleled Frankish trends, but tended to be lighter and less protective. Christian armies depended on the shock of the heavy cavalry charge, while Muslim armies relied on the fast wheeling attacks of the mounted horse archer."

The arms, armor, and tactics of the crusading armies and their Muslim adversaries underwent notable evolution over the two centuries of Christian occupation. Each camp influenced the other profoundly, borrowing and learning from each other. The Mongol hordes and the Byzantine armies also helped shape the costume and the operational art of war in the Latin kingdom.

European Arms and Armor

The warriors of the First Crusade looked scarcely different from the combatants at the Battle of Hastings in 1066. Most knights from Northern Europe wore a mail shirt or *hauberk*. European artisans produced excellent mail consisting of thousands of metal rings, each one linked to four others. Hauberks were mid-thigh in length and were usually worn over thick undershirts of leather or felt or padded garments stuffed with cotton. The *mail hauberk's* sleeves were loose, ending just below the elbow. The richer barons wore a mail sleeve under the hauberk to protect the lower arms, but many lesser knights left their forearms unprotected.

Mail was uncomfortably heavy on the wearer's shoulders, which supported the hanging weight of the iron shirt. Although mail provided great protection from the slashing blow, it was easy to penetrate with the point of a sword or a lance. Some knights wore double links at the price of flexibility, precisely to protect themselves from penetration from a thrusting blow. Temperatures that reached 100 degrees Fahrenheit required great endurance from soldiers wearing more than thirty pounds of mail over thickly padded garments underneath.

Knights from Italy often wore *scale* or *lamellar* armor, a practice borrowed from their Byzantine and Moorish North African neighbors. Plate 1 depicts a Siculo–Norman knight standing next to a crossbowman. Lamellar armor is worn around his torso as a *cuirass* or breastplate. Underneath he still wears a mail hauberk. The rectangular strips of the lamellar cuirass would have been made out of metal or cow horn, which made such a vest very light. His shoulders are protected by an early lamellar version of shoulder boards or *ailettes*. This would soon disappear but reemerge in the latter half of the thirteenth century among French knights.

Many warriors wore fabric body armor instead of or in addition to mail. These were called *aketons* or *gambesons*. They were made of multiple layers of cloth or two layers of buckram, a thick canvas, or coarse linen padded with cotton and rags. Either type was quilted vertically or in a crosshatched pattern to hold all in place. This type of armor works very much like a modern-day Kevlar vest. As the outer layers absorb a blow, the subsequent layers dissipate the perpendicular component of energy laterally, away from the body. *Aketons* were knee-length shirts with elbow-length sleeves and *gambesons* were shorter, reaching only the groin. Gambesons sometimes did not have sleeves, as can be seen on the crossbowman in Plate 1. Some aketons may have been lined with mail within their padded quilts, becoming versions of a Saracen *jazerant*.

Common foot soldiers wore mail or *scale armor* if their lords were wealthy or if they were resourceful enough to strip the dead friend or foe left on the many battlefields. Still, many set out without armor.

Coats of mail usually had an attached hood or *coif* that was secured to the head with a thong around it tied at the back. Over the coif, many wore simple conical *spangenhelm* helmets that were hammered from a single piece of metal reinforced by a band around the rim or assembled from plates hammered into shape, riveted together, and reinforced by metal strips covering the seams. A *nasal bard* was usually attached to protect the nose, but this device fell out of fashion by the mid-1100s. The helmets typically came to a shallow point at the apex. Among the Normans, the *Phrygian-shaped* helmet appeared popular, as pictured on the knight in Plate 1. This helmet with the apex of the cone bent slightly forward was borrowed from the conquered Saxons of England. Other helmet styles are shown in Plate 1, including the odd, high-topped version popular among German knights.

The *kite shield* was uniformly used by the cavalry. Its size and shape were designed to cover a rider's left side from shoulder to foot. A formal system of heraldry had not yet come into use, but these shields had individual decorations chosen by the owner. Made typically of linden wood or elm, it was covered with leather and lined with parchments on the inside. The man-at-arms carried the shield with forearm straps against a padded rest and an adjustable shoulder strap. The infantry used lighter, round shields or a flat-bottomed version of the kite shield that could easily be placed on the ground like later pavises.

The main weapon throughout the crusading era was the sword. The heavy *broadsword* favored by the mounted arm was double-edged with a slight taper from the hilt. The grips were formed by two carved pieces of wood assembled around the *tang*, wrapped with wire or leather thongs and topped with a round or ovoid pommel. The cross-guard or *quillons* were short and sometimes curved or bent downward. Roughly three feet long and weighing about four pounds, this weapon was capable of shearing a man in two from helmet to saddle.

The infantry needed a shorter sword and many carried a version of the *falchion*. This weapon developed from butchers' meat cleavers had a straight axis with a curving single-edge widening toward the tip.

The European mounted warrior's main weapon of attack was the *couched lance*, a narrow shaft of ash approximately ten feet in length in the early crusades, growing to around twelve feet in the latter years. A pennant was usually attached to the end of the lance, the tip of which sometimes sported a cross guard to prevent too deep a penetration as to prevent its withdrawal. The charge with a couched lance was enabled by the design of the knight's saddle, whose high cantle and pommel secured by double girths provided protective support front and back against the force of impact. The long stirrups allowed the rider to brace himself with a straight-legged posture as he charged.

Other infantry weapons are shown in Plate 1. The Normans adopted the great Anglo-Saxon *war axe* with a three-pound curved blade on a three-foot long shaft. Various versions of *maces* and *flails* were employed. In the early crusades, missile weapons consisted of the *shortbow*, which were simple bows from Northern Europe or Byzantine-style recurved bows, and the deadly *crossbow*.

Archers were capable of a high rate of fire, up to twelve shafts a minute, but the arrow was rarely capable of a mortal wound, especially at its extreme range of 250 yards. Crossbowmen launched a short, thick wooden bolt that could pierce body armor even at 200 yards. Its drawback was its slow rate of fire, hardly two bolts a minute with an expert. Early *crossbows* used a simple wood stave, but by the early 1200s, composite bows used whalebone sandwiched between pieces of yew and held together with glue and animal tendon. The greater power of later crossbows made them more difficult to span quickly.

Plate 2 depicts the evolution of European arms and armor in the twelfth century. Although the long, Norman kite shield continued to be in use by poorer knights and foot soldiers, the *heater-shaped* shield superceded it by the latter half of the century. The name coined by Victorian historians was derived from "heaters" or hand irons of the nineteenth century used to press clothing. The twelfth-century shields were still long by later standards, but the flat tops allowed the rider to see clearly over the edge. Italian soldiers continued to use a rectangular shield. Some infantry used the occasional round shield, many acquired from their Muslim adversaries.

Face masks replaced nasals on helmets by mid-century, and additional panels to protect the back of the neck led to full helmets that covered the entire head and neck in the latter decades. This design would culminate in the fully enclosed great helms of the thirteenth and fourteenth centuries. The most popular headgear for foot and mounted warriors was still a simple globular helmet called the *bascinet*. It was the custom to wear a bascinet under a mail coif. Swords, lances, and missile arms changed little through this period. A popular polearm among the foot soldiers was the *bill*, a military version of threshing pitchforks and scythes. *War picks* were used to penetrate the well-armored adversary's body defenses.

Mail armor now fully covered the limbs. Sleeves were worn tight with attached mail mittens and, early on, the shins were protected by mail. Later this would evolve into complete mail hose attached to a belt under the hauberk. Under their mail hauberks, Outremer knights of the twelfth century wore a long-skirted linen garment, colorfully printed in the Saracen manner. Returning crusaders popularized this fashion copied from Arab neighbors throughout Western Europe. This undergarment later became an outer coat or *surcoat* on which early heraldic devices would be emblazoned. The surcoat also served to protect the warrior encased in iron from the warming and eventually debilitating heat of the Middle Eastern sun.

Heraldry would not become a formal system until the mid-1200s, but in the late 1100s warriors would paint their distinctive badges on shields and helmets. The first formal royal coat of arms was Richard the Lionheart's two lions.

Horse armor had disappeared from use since the third century when Persian horsemen covered their horses with *trappers* of mail or lamellar armor. Earlier, Greeks and Romans protected their horses with *plates* covering the head and chest. In the 1100s, Christian horsemen began covering their horses with cloth or leather trappers to protect their mounts from spent arrows and easy hamstringing by enemy foot soldiers. Later, quilted barding and full mail *caparisons* were used. At the siege of Acre in 1191, a Saracen warrior reported with great awe the appearance of a Frankish knight on a horse covered to its hooves with mail *barding*.

Plate 3 shows examples of Christian equipment in the latter days of the Latin kingdom in the thirteenth century. Fully enclosing helmets quickly evolved into great helms with narrow eyeslits and small breathing holes. Many of these were gaily painted in the heraldic colors of the wearer. The discomfort of wearing a fully enclosed great helm led to the use of visors in the latter half of the 1200s. A popular alternative was the broad-brimmed *kettle hat* or *chapel-de-fer*.

Over the mail hauberk was worn a vest of metal plates or hardened leather panels to protect the upper torso, known as a *cuirie*, from the term *cuir bouilli*, leather hardened in boiling wax. (This term evolved in later centuries into cuirass, denoting any form of chest armor.) Quilted thigh defenses called cuisses became popular by mid-century. Additional protection was given the joints starting in mid-century. Squarish boards of cuir bouilli or metal called ailettes protected the shoulders. *Poleyns* protected the knees, growing from small saucer-shaped discs to larger bowls protecting even the sides of the joint by 1270. Around the same time, discs called *couters* protected the elbow.

The heater shield shrunk further, giving the knight less bulk to wield. The leather-covered wooden shields were now used to emblazon heraldry, which was now developing into a complex system of identification. Not much changed with the arms wielded by thirteenth century

Franks. Maces gained in popularity with both sides as armor improved. Though body and head armor became more impervious to penetration, a crushing blow with a heavy blunt instrument, such as a mace, still served to break bones and skulls.

Islamic Arms and Armor

Muslim armor paralleled Frankish trends, but tended to be lighter and less protective. Christian armies depended on the shock of the heavy cavalry charge, while Muslim armies relied on the fast wheeling attacks of the mounted horse archer. The Saracen emphasis on speed and quickness necessitated lighter body defenses. Throughout the two centuries of warfare, the Saracen horseman rarely wore leg and arm defenses.

A wider variety of armor styles existed among the Muslim communities. The most common body defense was a mail hauberk of varying lengths called a *dir*. The loose sleeves reached the elbow, leaving the forearms unprotected. Saracen hauberks had a stiffened collar to protect the neck. Mail was popular among the Egyptians and Arabs of Palestine.

Seljuk Turk warriors introduced the use of lamellar armor made of overlapping rows of small rectangular plates of metal, horn, or stiffened rawhide. This flexible body armor was typically stitched onto felt and was worn as a cuirass wrapped over the upper torso. Lamellar armor was in widespread use through several centuries. Later Muslims warriors, especially the Mamluks, wore a lamellar cuirass over their mail hauberks. Some suits of lamellar armor did include shoulder and upper arm protection in the form of hanging panels. Scale armor was a variant of lamellar armor usually worn by heavy cavalry.

Helmets were of the simple conical egg shape or *baida*. These were simple or gilded and inscribed with Koranic verses. Additional mail, leather, or lamellar panels to protect the ears and neck were added. Other versions were hammered as one piece with the base of the helmet. It was a fairly common practice among elite cavalrymen, the Mamluks or the Turkish *askaris*, to wear a veil of mail attached to the helmet so as to cover the entire head except for the eyes. This fashion was not widespread among Arab warriors. In the twelfth century, mail *aventails* attached to the brim of the helmets was popularized by Persian elite warriors.

Light cavalry and infantry wore minimal armor and sometimes wore no body defenses at all. Quilted or padded fabric body armor, some lined with a layer of mail, may have been a standard among some light cavalry contingents and better-equipped infantry.

Saracen swords were descended from Byzantine and Roman designs. Until the latter half of the thirteenth century, most Arab warriors used straight double-edged swords similar to the crusaders' but narrower with less of a taper and a short cross guard. Seljuk Turks and Persians wielded narrow swords with a very slight curve and a slanted hilt. A sword knot made of a decorative cord with tasseled ends was copied from the Persians and prevented the loss of one's sword in battle or the chase. It was only with the arrival of the Mongols in the mid-1200s that the curved *saber* and *scimitar* came into wide use. Axes and maces were favorite sidearms. Many Saracen nobles owned prized swords and axes with inlaid designs or intricate metalwork, many of which survive to the present day. Damascus was the recognized cradle of such beautiful designs. The Damascene blade was indeed a treasure sought after and envied.

The Saracen cavalryman was first and foremost a horse archer dependent upon a recurved *composite bow* three to four feet in length, made of layers of horn, wood, and sinew. A quiver containing thirty arrows of various types was usually hung on a belt on the rider's right side or slung over the shoulder on a strap. The bow was carried in a case on the rider's left. At least six types of arrows were known, each used depending on whether the target had a shield or wore mail or lamellar plate armor. The arrow was lethal only at close range.

It was not uncommon for Muslim cavalry to carry spears, but these were used more as throwing *javelins* or overhand *prickers* than as couched lances. In the early years, these lances were about seven feet long, but as more battles were fought with the European knights, these lances grew in length and girth. When used as couched lances, the earlier spears, some of which were of bamboo, broke easily before penetrating body armor. After the Third Crusade, Saracen cavalry used thicker lances in imitation of the Franks. Still, the Muslim horse warrior preferred not to engage in jousts.

Saracen infantry were lightly armed and armored. Foot archers went to battle without any mail or lamellar protection, armed with longer *"self"* bows. These consisted of staves, around five feet in length, of simpler construction, some being reinforced with horn in the middle section. Although some foot soldiers wore simple helmets, the greater number merely donned turbans, or in the case of Turkish warriors, simple peaked fur-lined hats called *kalaftahs*. A few wore lamellar or scale armor or a captured mail hauberk stripped from a dead crusader.

Crossbows were usually obtained by capture or through trading with the Italians, especially the Genoese, who made the best examples and were expert in their use. Crossbows were not used extensively in the open field battles, being quite slow to fire, but found good use in defending fortifications and camps from besiegers.

Round shields were the norm for both infantry and cavalry. As with European shields, these were made of wood polished or covered with leather with a metal strip on the outer edge. The occasional kite shield was also used by Muslim warriors, copied or obtained from Byzantine Varangian guards, many of whom were, in fact, displaced Normans. Foot soldiers used kite shields with flat bottoms well into the thirteenth century. Long ovoid shields were also used by infantry. By the thirteenth century, some Mamluk horsemen used *heater shields* copied from the Europeans.

There is little evidence that horse armor was used by Arab armies in the late eleventh century. Elite Seljuk horsemen invading from the east did protect their mares with lamellar panels in the Persian manner. By the mid-twelfth century, cloth or quilted coverings or caparisons began to appear on the mounts of both sides. The Saracen armies, however, preferred to keep their mounts minimally burdened and lightly protected because mobility and quickness were essential to an effective sally by horse archers. Armored horses were used by the few heavy shock cavalry employed in Saracen armies.

Plate 4 shows a heavy Seljuk cavalryman of the late eleventh century, well protected with a *scale armor* cuirass and a helmet with full enclosure of mail to protect the face, head, and neck. His arms are also fully protected. Standing next to him is a light cavalryman who appears to wear no armor at all. Muslim clothing was generally loose and comfortable, and contemporary depictions of light cavalry do not show much evidence of extensive mail or lamellar protection beneath the light cloth of their garments.

Plate 5 portrays the evolution of Saracenic armor in the twelfth century. A Turkish crossbowman wearing a *kalaftah helmet* stands next to a heavy cavalryman whose horse is protected by a short *mail trapper*. The cavalryman's helmet's "face" visor is Byzantine in origin. Although the horseman is clearly a "heavy" cavalryman, evidenced by his elaborate scale and mail armor and his long lance, he is still armed with a bow and arrow and his leg defenses are quite minimal.

A fully armed Mamluk heavy cavalryman of the last years of the Latin kingdom is shown in Plate 6 beside a light cavalryman and a foot soldier. The curved Mongol-style saber depicted in this plate would become the preferred blade of the Middle Eastern warrior in the following centuries. A lamellar cuirass with a mail hauberk underneath serves to protect the heavy cavalryman. His helmet sports a movable visor; his forearms are protected by plate and his legs by mail. His companion on horseback is a typical Mamluk ghulam, lightly armored with a lamellar cuirass but lacking limb defenses. It is notable that the heavy cavalryman can easily be mistaken for a crusader by his caparisoned horse, his heater shield, and his heavy armor. This perception is, however, betrayed by the bow and arrow quiver he carries.

The crusaders were awed by a uniquely Saracen weapon they called Greek fire and the Arabs referred to as naphtha. Large flaming balls launched from catapults and other medieval artillery rained upon them. Arab grenadiers also hurled these mixtures contained in small pots of clay or glass jars. The exact composition has been lost, but one easily surmises that it was made with the oil tar and petroleum abundant in some areas. Because the payloads were sticky and ignited with water, sulfur and quicklime would have been added. At the first siege of Mansourah, the fiery missiles hurled by a battery of sixteen catapults turned night into day around the terrified crusader encampment.

Organization

The European and Saracen armies mirrored each other in their dependence on feudal levies built around a small cadre of elite fighting men. The Muslim armies were better organized in specific regiments and defined chains of command. Christian armies reflected the ad hoc nature of European feudal forces, with contingents of varying sizes taking orders only from their liege lords.

The Christian Armies

The king of Jerusalem in theory controlled all the lands of Outremer and parceled portions to various barons in return for a commitment to provide warriors for the defense of the kingdom. The fact that the king assumed power by consent of the barons diluted his authority on the battlefield. Some barons withheld their own forces or barred passage of the royal regiments through their lands if they disagreed with the king's policies. The fatal equivocation by King Guy at Hattin was the result of having to listen to competing factions of Outremer nobility.

When new armies arrived from Europe, their leaders assumed that theirs was the commander's role and seldom heeded the advice and needs of the local military leadership. When one leader with tactical sense asserted himself, as Richard the Lionheart did, the Christian armies had a chance of prevailing. When battlefield command was ill defined as at Damascus and Hattin, the result was disaster. Unity of command was no guarantee of success, however. Operational acumen was the key; witness the inept but assertive Cardinal Pelagius' debacle at Mansourah.

The closest thing to a Christian elite were the military orders whose rigid chains of command and systematic martial training provided the kingdom with regular regiments. However, each order was self-contained and answered only to its own hierarchy. The Christian commanders had to negotiate for their order's participation in campaigns and had to acquiesce to battlefield orders.

The Christian armies were very much loose alliances always on the verge of fracturing. Command and control were short-lived. In the later years as crusading fervor ebbed, the various European kingdoms financed the hiring of mercenaries whose loyalty and control were assured as long as they could count on being paid. Professional infantry from Brittany, the counties of the Netherlands, and even Aragon saw service in the Holy Land, along with professional Italian crossbowmen.

Muslim Armies

Muslim rulers gripped power with a small but well-organized palace guard. The Abbasid caliph in Baghdad was considered first among equals in the

Muslim world. His bodyguard was a structured organization whose members drew salaries from the government. This imperial guard, comprised mostly of Turks, was divided into distinct units of cavalry, heavy infantry, and archers. Specialized companies of naphtha-hurling grenadiers and engineers were an essential part of this compact regiment of no more than five thousand.

In times of war, tribal levies, volunteers, and mercenaries from Persia, Africa, Greece, and even Western Europe, were organized around this elite corps of well-trained and educated warriors. The caliph could then field large armies organized into decimal subdivisions; a corps of ten thousand commanded by an emir was comprised of regiments of one thousand, companies of one hundred, and sections of ten men.

The Turkish Imperial Guard's power grew over the centuries such that the caliphs became puppets of their own generals. The caliph's diminution was further exacerbated by the implementation of the *Iqta*, the system wherein local emirs took on the payment of their own forces. The inability of the impoverished caliphate in the latter half of the eleventh century to maintain its garrisons diluted its sovereignty, as the richer emirs drew power from what became their private armies. The Seljuk Turks began their conquest of Saracen lands in the eleventh century when they were invited into Baghdad to assist the caliph who suspected the vizier of his Imperial Guard of sedition.

The other Saracen caliphates and sultanates also depended on a palace guard to maintain power. When the Seljuks enjoyed their zenith, the sultan's mounted bodyguard regiment called the askar was his source of power. The emirs who owed him fealty had their own askars as well. An askar was made up of approximately two thousand or so askaris who at any time were of Turkish, Byzantine, Slavic, or Frank descent. In war, the various askars of the emirs united under the sultan's banner. Eventually, the competition among the powerful emirs tore the Seljuk empire apart, with the sultan again becoming a mere figurehead.

The Egyptian Fatimid caliphs fielded the largest armies in the region. The caliph's elite bodyguard of white slaves from northern climes and Sudanese infantry formed his core strength. The mounted arm was organized into regiments identified by the race of its members, e.g., the Slav, Armenian, Byzantine, Black, or Sudanese regiments. Wartime brought mercenaries, levies, and the contingents of vassal emirs into large coalitions that reflected the wealth and reach of the Fatimid empire.

The Fatimid armies were unique among the Saracens for their lack of mounted archers, relying instead on a core of heavy cavalry that were no match for armored Frankish knights and vast numbers of light cavalry.

The Egyptian navy was the only powerful armada in the Muslim world and was a constant threat to the Christian flotillas. The marines on board were often used in land operations.

In 1169, Saladin overthrew the Fatimid vizier and cruelly quelled the Black regiment's uprising. Thus began the Ayyubid dynasty. He immediately reconstituted the palace guard using his own Kurdish horsemen and askars from Damascus. The armies he led against the Latin kingdom were augmented with mercenaries and feudal levies from emirates now sworn to jihad. Saladin's constant challenge was to keep his feudal troops in the field during long campaigns. It was their custom to return home after a few weeks. Still, the imperative of jihad enabled Saladin to keep his army intact on a continuous campaign of three years (1190–1193). His army resembled those of the Seljuks with the emphasis on the use of mounted archers as the arbiters of battle.

After Saladin, the Ayyubid sultans grew weaker and increasingly suspected their own bodyguards of disloyalty. They imported new slaves from the Turkish and Armenian north to form new personal askars. From them developed the powerful caste of Mamluks who took power from their masters in 1250.

The Mamluk armies were more aggressive and ferocious than any previous Saracen force. Their pedigree as disciplined units raised and trained from boyhood to be elite warriors was incomparable for the era. Their steely professionalism stiffened the backs of the levies and mercenaries that fought alongside them.

Horse archers still dominated the main force of the Mamluk armies, but heavy cavalry units armed with lances and mounted on barded horses were now a potent force. The use of grenadiers armed with Greek fire grenades continued. A Mamluk army on the move enjoyed an efficient logistics chain of camel caravans and depots of food and supplies on the route. Baybars linked the garrisons of his kingdom with a system of dispatch riders on well-maintained roads. The health of the soldiers was maintained by a dedicated corps of physicians and chemists who dispensed drugs to treat diseases before they became epidemics.

Mamluk sultans loved their bands and lesser emirs craved the royal commission to have their own drum, hautboys, and trumpet ensembles. The incessant beating of drums during a battle with the Mamluks served to disconcert their enemies. Command and control was exercised through a system of drumbeats and flags.

Tactics

It is very easy to depict medieval battles as mere disorganized melees of spearing, slashing, and hacking. Though this may have been true of the climactic phases of most battles, unique tactical doctrines were employed by both sides in the encounter and engagement phases. Over the two centuries of warfare, tactics evolved on both sides as each learned from the other.

The centerpiece of European tactical doctrine was the charge of the *conrois*, closely packed lines of armored knights with couched lances riding stirrup to stirrup. The infantry, consisting of archers and spearmen, served to screen the mounted knights until the charge was ordered. It was rare that infantry were used in the attack. The foot soldiers screened the horsemen before they charged and to provide secure lines they could retire behind upon returning.

Cavalry was organized into squadrons of approximately one hundred men. An army was typically divided into three battles or divisions, each of which had several squadrons. The cavalry of each battle were arranged in three lines. The first line was a position of honor consisting of the wealthier knights, the other two lines made up of poorer knights and men-at-arms. The squadrons rarely charged as one body, but were sent by the battle commander against different sectors of the enemy's lines of battle. The commander of the battle usually stayed with the third and last line. Once that line charged, there was little control he could exercise on the progress of the battle.

The ideals of chivalry requiring individual glory on the battlefield were the bane of a Christian military commander. The knight's first instinct was to charge an enemy as soon as he was in sight, and many new arrivals did so to the chagrin of the local veterans. Tactical control of formations and coordination of attacks were never simple tasks. At Mansourah, King

Louis IX's brother's insistence to attack the fortified town well ahead of the main body led to his destruction along with hundreds of Templars and English crusaders.

Muslim tactics varied slightly from one group to another, but with the exception of the Egyptian Fatimids, were uniformly built around the use of masses of mounted archers on speedy horses releasing a storm of arrows on the enemy. Under the torrent of missiles, the enemy would be herded into an ever-tightening circle. When the enemy cavalry sallied forth to attack, the Saracen cavalry would retreat, drawing the enemy's horsemen farther from the protection of their main lines. As soon as the enemy began to return to their positions on tired horses, the Saracen cavalry reserve would attack, cutting off the spent force.

The first encounter showed each side the strengths and weaknesses of the other's tactics. Time and again, the Frankish conrois could not engage the fast-riding Saracens on their quick mares. The result was helpless attrition under the arrow storm. Still, the Saracen light cavalry could not overrun well-deployed Christian infantry and instead continued pouring arrows on the tightly packed masses. Whenever Muslim riders were trapped, as at Dorylaeum when a second crusader column caught the Seljuks surrounding Bohemond's camp on weary horses, the power of the charging knight was unstoppable and the slaughter was complete.

In future battles, the Franks learned to avoid encirclement by keeping a reserve force away from the main body or by using the topography of the battlefield, wisely anchoring their flanks on natural obstacles such as elevated ground, forest, or water. If at all possible, they charged the horse archers before they could form up.

The Saracens learned their lessons well. They would avoid any contact with the Christian cavalry until victory was certain, use the mobility of their horse archers to harass and separate the infantry from the horsemen, pick off stragglers, isolate the rearguard, and when the enemy's formations were broken, press home with a charge of lance and sword. If the enemy's heavy cavalry broke out of line with a charge of lances, the Muslim light cavalry was instructed to attack the flanks to surround and isolate the knights. Conscious effort was made to keep the crusaders from sources of water. These were Saladin's tactics at Hattin and Arsuf.

To counter these tactics, the Franks instilled discipline on the march, demanding that each man keep his assigned place in line regardless of any sallies by Saracen horse archers. The military orders expelled any of their members who abandoned place in rank without permission. On a march, several formations were maintained. In open country, the army traveled in a square formation, each side prepared to respond to any attack. In narrow areas, columns were maintained, with the infantry screening the cavalry and the baggage train. Richard the Lionheart marched his army in such formations while Saladin's horse archers rode up and down Richard's columns pestering the Christians with arrows.

Egyptian Fatimid armies mirrored the Frankish forces in general organization and tactics. They had little dependence on mounted archery. The Christian armies invariably triumphed because the Fatimid cavalryman tended to meet his counterpart head on, but lacked the armor to withstand the Frankish lances. If the Christian charge happened to hit the center of gravity of the Egyptian lines, the Fatimids collapsed easily, as happened at Ramleh in 1101 when, on the verge of defeat, King Baldwin charged the center of the Egyptian line with the remaining half of his cavalry.

The Egyptians' superior numbers were sometimes too much to overcome and mounted charges against them served to only hasten the end. At the second battle of Ramleh in 1102, Baldwin lost his small force of five hundred cavalry after many furious charges against an encircling Fatimid army of twenty thousand. The same catastrophe befell the army of Antioch at the Field of Blood in 1119.

Saladin converted the Egyptian army to the horse archer-centered Turkish model inherited by the Arabs. These tactical doctrines reached their pinnacle with the Mamluks. Relying on the feint and false withdrawal, the Mamluks scored their greatest victory against the Mongols at Ayn Jalut. They used their favorite tactic of the nighttime mounted raid in their unrelenting reconquest of Christian redoubts and towns. By the time the last frantic boatload of Christians departed Acre in 1291, the Mamluks were a complete military machine, dominant in all phases of the operational art.

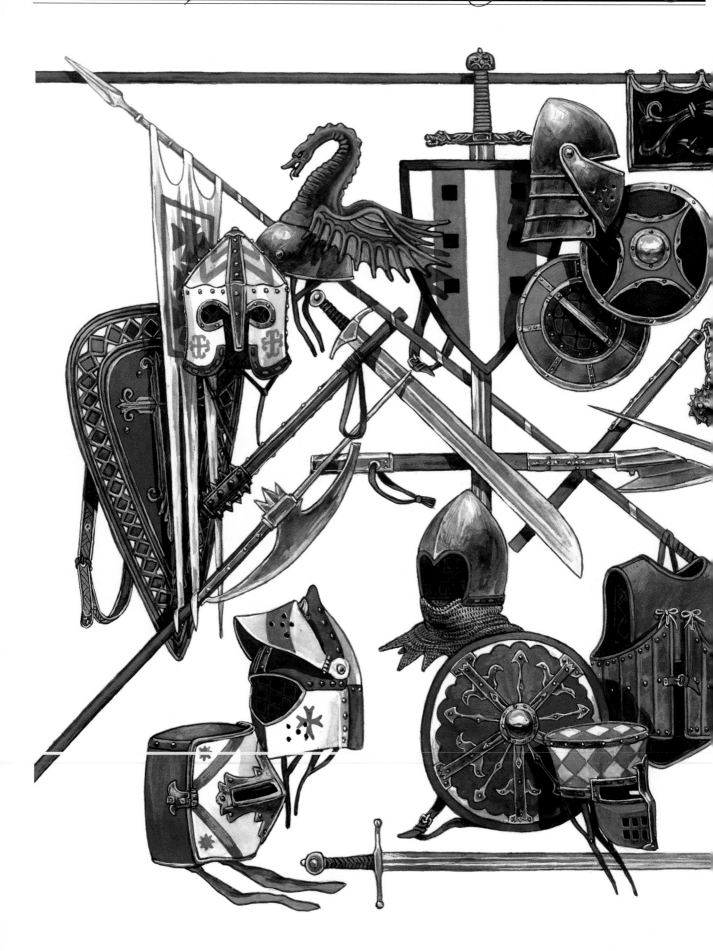

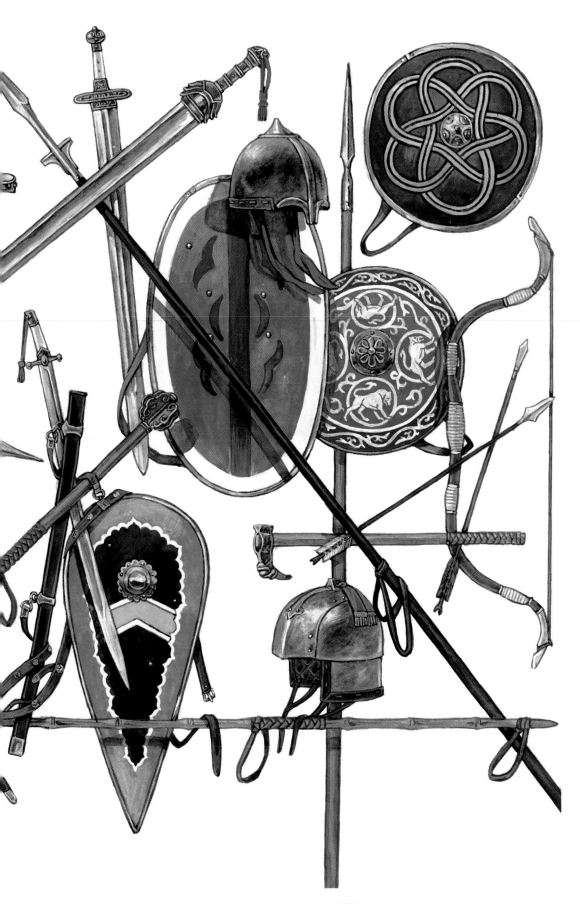

Plate 5. Saracen Arms and Armor of the 12th Century

King Richard the Lionheart

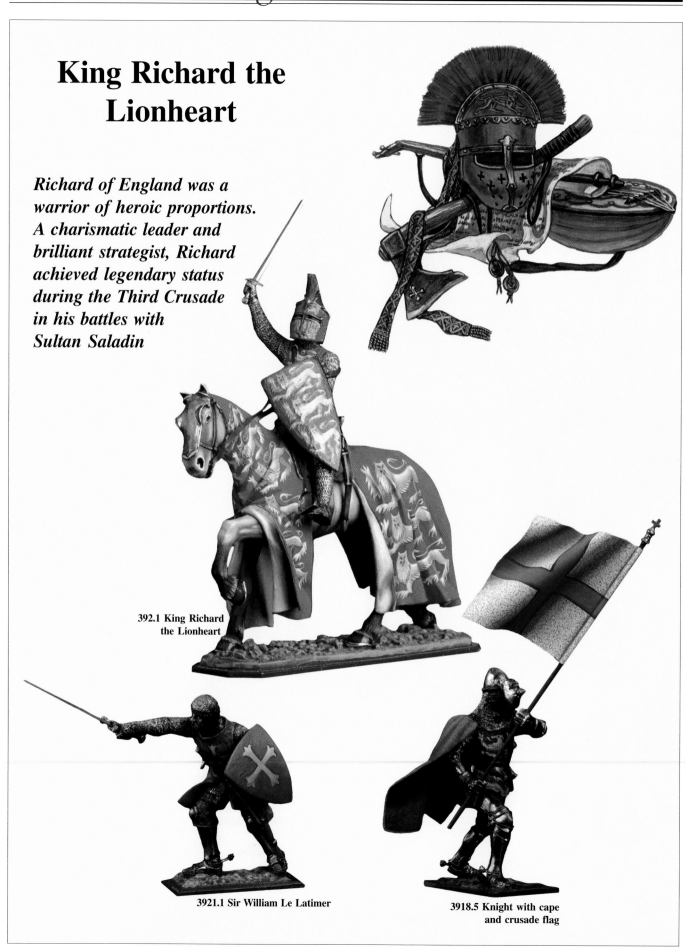

Richard of England was a warrior of heroic proportions. A charismatic leader and brilliant strategist, Richard achieved legendary status during the Third Crusade in his battles with Sultan Saladin

392.1 King Richard the Lionheart

3921.1 Sir William Le Latimer

3918.5 Knight with cape and crusade flag

Knights Templar

Knights of the Temple of Soloman, or Templars, were dedicated to protection of poor pilgrims traveling to and from the Holy Land and became the most powerful of the military orders in the 12th and 13th centuries.

3932.3 Templar Knight with French flag

3928.2 Knight Templar kneeling with crossbow

3701 Battle weary crusader with sword and flag

5009.1 Templar fighting with axe

3123.4 Knight Templar with axe

Knights Hospitallers

The Hospitallers of St. John of Jerusalem became the longest-lived of the monks of war, surviving the crusades to battle the Ottoman Turks in the 15th and 16th centuries.

3701 Battle weary Knight Hospitaller with flag

5009.1 Knight Hospitaller fighting with axe

5009.2 Knight Hospitaller fighting with sword and shield

5009.3 Knight Hospitaller charging with flag

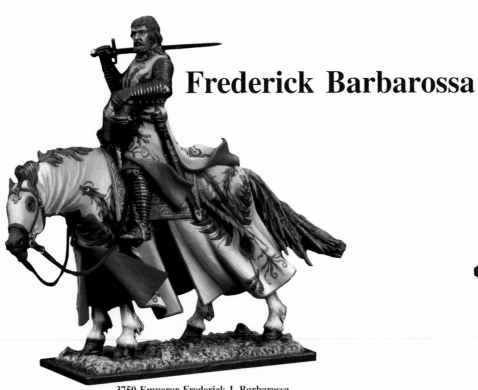

Frederick Barbarossa

3933.1 German Knight
charging with axe

3750 Emperor Frederick I, Barbarossa

Emperor Frederick I was one of the most powerful and able of the medieval rulers as well as a great warrior. He died at age 68 while on the Third Crusade.

ME14 German Man-at-arms with flag

Teutonic Knights

The Order of Teutonic Knights was established in the 12th century under the jurisdiction of a Grand Master (Hochmeister). This order of German knights went on to battle in Russia and Eastern Europe before being defeated by the Poles at Grunwald in 1410.

379.4 Teutonic Knight with sword

PB24.1 13th Century Teutonic Knight

3184.2 Teutonic Knight with cape and sword

3933.3 Teutonic Knight, charging with flag of Grand Master

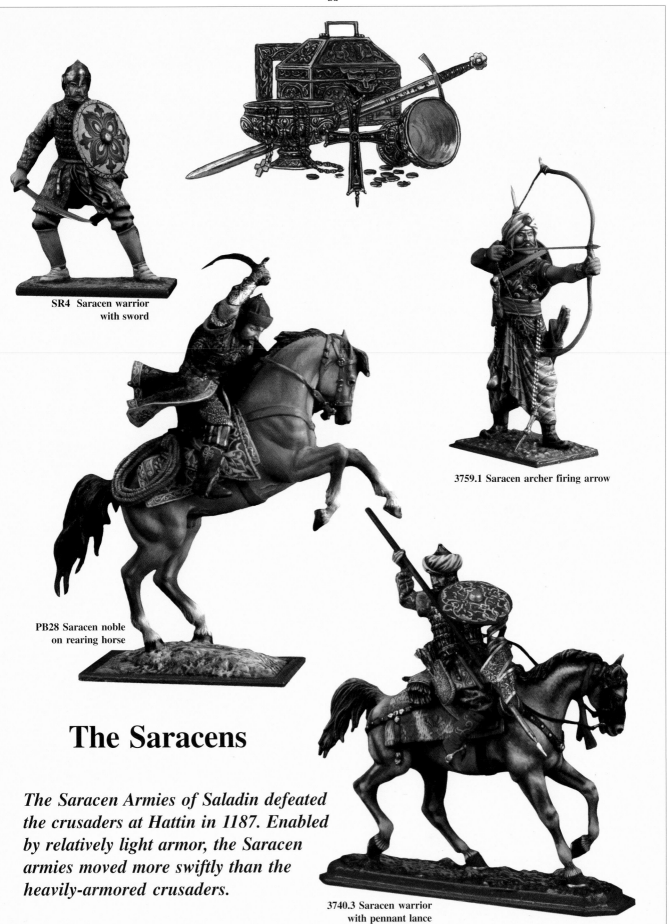

SR4 Saracen warrior
with sword

3759.1 Saracen archer firing arrow

PB28 Saracen noble
on rearing horse

The Saracens

*The Saracen Armies of Saladin defeated
the crusaders at Hattin in 1187. Enabled
by relatively light armor, the Saracen
armies moved more swiftly than the
heavily-armored crusaders.*

3740.3 Saracen warrior
with pennant lance

BIBLIOGRAPHY

Billings, Malcolm. *The Cross and the Crescent*. New York: Sterling, 1987.

Hallam, Elizabeth, ed. *Chronicles of the Crusades*. New York: Weidenfeld and Nicolson, 1989.

Heath, Ian. *Armies and Enemies of the Crusades 1096–1291 A.D.* Dallas, TX: Wargames Research Group, 1978.

Jones, Terry, and Alan Ereira. *Crusades*. New York: Facts on File, 1995.

Konstam, Angus. *Historical Atlas of the Crusades*. New York: Thalmus, 2002.

Lamb, Harold. *The Crusades, Iron Men and Saints*. Garden City, New York: Doubleday, Doran & Company, 1930.

Lamb, Harold. *The Crusades, The Flame of Islam*. Garden City, New York: Doubleday, Doran & Company, 1931.

Madden, Thomas F. *A Concise History of the Crusades*. Lanham, MD: Rowan & Littlefield, 1999.

Mayer, L. A. *Saracenic Heraldry*. New York: Oxford Press, 1999.

Miller, David. *Brasseys Book of the Crusades*. Washington, DC: Brasseys, 2001.

Nicolle, David. *Arms and Armor of the Crusading Era 1050–1350 A.D.* New York: Osprey, 1988.

Nicolle, David. *Saracen Faris 1050–1250 A.D.* London: Osprey, 1994.

Nicolle, David. *The Mamluks 1250–1517*. London: Osprey, 1993.

Nicolle, David. *The Knights of Outremer 1187–1344 A.D.* London: Osprey, 1996.

Norwich, John Julius. *Byzantinium, the Decline and Fall*. New York: Alfred A. Knopf, 1996.

Prawer, Joshua. *The World of the Crusades*. New York: Quadrangle Books, 1972.

Runciman, S. *A History of the Crusades*. 3 vols. Cambridge, England: Cambridge University Press, 1988.

Seward, Desmond. *The Monks of War*. London: Eyre Methuen, 1972.

Wise, Terence. *The Armies of the Crusades*. London: Osprey, 1978.

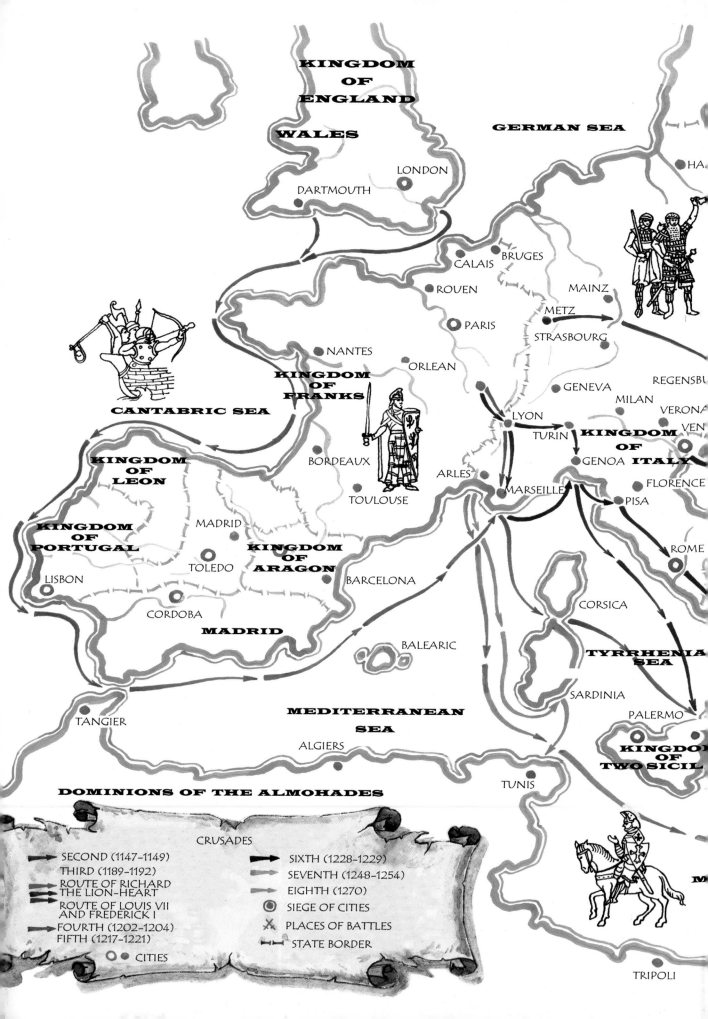

KINGDOM OF ENGLAND

WALES

LONDON

DARTMOUTH

GERMAN SEA

HA

BRUGES

CALAIS

ROUEN

MAINZ

METZ

PARIS

STRASBOURG

NANTES

ORLEAN

KINGDOM OF FRANKS

REGENSBU

GENEVA

MILAN

VERONA

CANTABRIC SEA

LYON

KINGDOM OF ITALY

TURIN

VEN

KINGDOM OF LEON

BORDEAUX

ARLES

GENOA

KINGDOM OF PORTUGAL

MADRID

TOULOUSE

MARSEILLE

FLORENCE

PISA

ROME

TOLEDO

KINGDOM OF ARAGON

LISBON

BARCELONA

CORSICA

CORDOBA

MADRID

BALEARIC

TYRRHENIA SEA

SARDINIA

MEDITERRANEAN SEA

PALERMO

TANGIER

ALGIERS

KINGDO OF TWO SICIL

TUNIS

DOMINIONS OF THE ALMOHADES

M

TRIPOLI